"A small treasure-house of beauty and imagination, helping us in turn to imagine God's world and God's love with multi-faceted and grateful wisdom."
—N. T. WRIGHT, Professor Emeritus of New Testament, University of St Andrews

"Have you ever feared that rational, duty-bound thinking is the best you can do to invite God's presence in your life? Malcolm Guite stoutly defends the divinely operating faculty of the enlivened imagination as a magnifying glass to bring divine grace into focus for those willing to open the heart and mind to imagery and poetry."
—LUCI SHAW, author *The O in Hope* and *Angels Everywhere*

"There is a sense in which we live between worlds—on the one hand a realm of broken symmetry, loss, pain, and death; on the other that of beauty, of love and the soaring realm of the redeemed senses. We catch glimpses of that 'other country' via the imagination, and like the famous Inklings C.S. Lewis, Charles Williams, and J.R.R. Tolkien, the poet Malcolm Guite helps us to pull back the scrim of appearances in order to see the large and startling world in which we actually live. The redeemed imagination is an organ of insight—as the poet shows us in lucid and lucent manner."
—BRUCE HERMAN, artist and Lothlórien Distinguished Chair in Fine Arts, Gordon College

"This is an important book, a necessary book, reclaiming for the noetic imagination its due appreciation as a means of apprehending truth."
—SCOTT CAIRNS, author of *Slow Pilgrim*

"I hear people ask all the time: 'Why? Why imagination matter?' and now I have *Liftin* In this short, elegant, accessible book Mac those questions to the mat and pins them there, revealing the imagination as the fundamental engine of insight, wisdom, and, ultimately, hope itself. Everyone should read this book."
—A. S. PETERSON, author and director of Rabbit Room Press

"*Lifting the Veil* is beautifully written as well as visually engaging. This compilation achieves accessibility without sacrificing an ounce of depth—a rare feat. I'll be recommending this book to visual artists and poetry lovers alike."
—LAWAN GLASSCOCK, Christians in the Visual Arts (CIVA)

"*Lifting the Veil* is like Boethius' *Consolation* and Dante's *Vita nova,* a splendid mix of prose and poetry, but with even more kenosis and humility as Malcolm Guite includes the poetry of others, not just his own. His voices become the Good Shepherd, the Good Samaritan, resonating so with Christ's Bible, along with a great Cloud of Witnesses, Coleridge, Herbert, Langland, Blake and more. Like George Fox, he sees that of God in everyone. He rightfully argues for poetry as theology. Dante built his new Jerusalem as Florence, Guite as England, both as the Cosmos."

—JULIA BOLTON HOLLOWAY, author of *Julian of Norwich: Showing of Love, Extant Texts and Translation*

"Malcolm Guite enjoins us to apprehend the powerful witness and conjuring of the Kingdom that is the work of what C.S. Lewis called a 'baptised Imagination.' Replete with beautifully striking black and white prints from the history of the Christian tradition and the present, this little book allows word and image to commune together. *Lifting the Veil* is a gem of a book that piques the very imagination it seeks to address."

—RACHEL HOSTETTER SMITH, art historian and president of the Association of Scholars of Christianity in the History of Art (ASCHA)

"I spent my childhood more present in the world of the imagination than in the physical world, hopelessly drawn to wonder, beauty, and story, but the churches I grew up in had no theology of wonder-hunger. It wasn't until my late twenties that I realized all those poetic longings must ultimately be met and answered in the person of a Creator who must then necessarily be more wonderful and beautiful, and more of a poet than ever I had been taught. God bless Malcolm Guite for thinking through and articulating for the rest of us the ways in which the imagination is not just a valid, but a vital part of the life of a Christ-follower. May this book open to others a more robust theology of the imagination than was available to me when I was younger."

—DOUGLAS MCKELVEY, author of *Every Moment Holy*

"Written with an old soul, Malcolm Guite's *Lifting The Veil* invites us to cultivate our imagination to awaken our spiritual affections. Drawing from the words and life of Jesus, the Scriptures, poetry, and visual images, Guite invites us to make new stories, stories that surprise us with God's truth. Malcolm Guite offers us all a prophetic encouragement in this beautiful book."

—SANDRA MCCRACKEN, singer-songwriter, hymn writer, and author of *Send Out Your Light: The Illuminating Power of Scripture and Song*

LIFTING *the* VEIL

Imagination and the Kingdom of God

LIFTING *the* VEIL

Imagination and the Kingdom of God

MALCOLM GUITE

SQUARE HALO BOOKS

In Christian art, the square halo identified a living person presumed to be a saint. Square Halo Books is devoted to publishing works that present contextually sensitive biblical studies, and practical instruction consistent with the Doctrines of the Reformation. The goal of Square Halo Books is to provide materials useful for encouraging and equipping the saints.

The art on the cover is *Jacob's Ladder,*
or *Jacob's Dream* by William Blake (front)
and *Good Friday in One Thousand Places*
by Bruce Herman (back).

©2021 Square Halo Books, Inc.
P.O. Box 18954
Baltimore, MD 21206
www.SquareHaloBooks.com

All Scripture quotations, unless otherwise indicated, are taken from the Holy Bible, New Revised Standard Version.

ISBN 978-1-941106-22-8
Library of Congress Control Number: 2021939467

Printed in the United States of America

For Jeremy Begbie:
*Teacher, Friend,
and Scholar*

Acknowledgments

LIFTING THE VEIL developed out of "Imagining the Kingdom," the three Laing Lectures I gave at Regent College, Vancouver, in 2019. I would like to thank Regent for doing me the great honour of inviting me to be the Laing Lecturer, and to thank Roger and Carol Laing for their foresight and generosity in founding the lectureship in honour of their father William John Laing. The community of Christian writers, thinkers, artists, and teachers which has gathered around Regent College over the years has been very important to me and has nurtured and sharpened my vocation as a Christian poet.

I am also grateful to Square Halo Books for taking on this project and in particular to Ned Bustard for his help, guidance, many useful suggestions, and wonderful selection of art, as we worked together to turn the original lectures into a substantial and beautifully illustrated book which we hope will help to guide and inspire a new generation of Christian artists.

I am grateful to Luci Shaw, Richard Hays, Canterbury Press, The C.S. Lewis Estate, and Macmillan Publishers for permission to quote some of the poems and prose extracts in this book.

I am, as always, deeply indebted to my friend and amanuensis Judith Tonry, to my personal assistant Philippa Pearson, and to my patient and encouraging wife Maggie.

Finally I would like to thank Jeremy Begbie, to whom this book is dedicated for setting me on a path, many years ago, which has led me deep into the nurturing and refreshing realm of Theology and the Arts.

CONTENTS

The Creation, an engraving by William Blake from *Illustrations of the Book of Job*.

IMAGINATION
and the
KINGDOM
OF GOD

THIS BOOK IS A DEFENSE of the imagination as a truth-bearing faculty, and more than that it is an appeal to artists, poets, sculptors, storytellers, and filmmakers to kindle our imaginations for Christ, who is himself the kindling imagination of God, who brings all things into being. In our compartmentalized, privatized, individualized, and divided world, the arts have been relegated to something purely subjective, a matter of individual taste, a decorative version of "what's true for me," a private aesthetic thrill to compensate for the grimness of what is actually out there, something to numb the mind as it faces the brutality of day-to-day living. Such is the view today, and it is the exact opposite of how the arts and artists were once seen and could be seen again. Far from numbing the mind or turning our gaze inwards to the merely private and subjective, Samuel Taylor Coleridge, the great poet and theologian of the imagination, says that he and William Wordsworth were using the arts to *awaken the mind's attention*, to help us, just as much as science might help us, to look out and see what is really there and to discover that reality is itself numinous, translucent with glimmerings of the "supernatural," of something holy shining through it. Here is what Coleridge says about their intentions in writing *Lyrical Ballads*:

to excite a feeling analogous to the supernatural, by awakening the mind's attention to the lethargy of custom, and directing it to the loveliness and the wonders of the world before us; an inexhaustible treasure, but for which, in consequence of the film of familiarity and selfish solicitude, we have eyes, yet see not, ears that hear not, and hearts that neither feel nor understand.[1]

Central to this passage is the idea of "the film of familiarity and selfish solicitude." Coleridge says that it is as though there were a film or veil between us and the radiant reality of things. This film is not there by accident: we have put it there! We have dulled our own vision of the world, both by over-familiarity and by what Coleridge calls "selfish solicitude," that is to say, we are treating nature not only as a familiar and easily dismissible background but also as an agglomeration of *stuff* for us to exploit. That is what *selfish solicitude* means, it means we *solicit* or demand from the world all its goods and resources for our own selfish ends, without considering its own intrinsic being or purpose. To make that exploitation easier, to avoid being challenged by the radiant beauty and otherness of nature, we throw over it this "film of familiarity and selfish solicitude." Then, because of what Coleridge calls the *lethargy of custom*, we forget that the veil, the film of familiarity is there at all, and think that nature is as dull as we are. The whole purpose of the arts, not just poetry but all the arts, is to *awaken the mind's attention* to remove "the film of familiarity," to "cleanse the doors of perception" as Blake put it. The power which art deploys to do these things is the power of imagination. There is a paradox here. We have come to think of the imagination as merely about the *imaginary*, about making things up, and we can of course make things up, but paradoxically, even as we do, we find new ways of glimpsing and telling the truth. As Coleridge says slightly earlier in the same passage, about his own imaginary stories like "The Rime of the Ancient Mariner":

> ... my endeavors should be directed to persons and characters supernatural, or at least romantic; yet so as to transfer from our inward nature a human interest and a semblance of truth sufficient to procure for these shadows of imagination that willing suspension of disbelief for the moment, which constitutes poetic faith.[2]

We can all think of times when imaginary stories—parables, myths and legends, novels, and films have suddenly awoken our minds to important truths we had missed or had been denying. But there is more: the power of imagination does not just come into play when we are making up stories, it is the imagination which allows us to grasp the whole, the meaning, the pattern in what we perceive, to draw the lines that connects the dots, to glimpse the pattern that suddenly makes sense of disparate and apparently random things. It is by the forming and perceiving power of imagination that the constant stream of data flowing into us through our senses is shaped into a tree, a mountain, a sunset, the face of our beloved. Indeed, in Coleridge's *Biographia Literaria*, in the chapter just before the passages we have just quoted, he goes so far to say that:

> The primary IMAGINATION I hold to be the living Power and prime
> Agent of all human Perception, and as a repetition in the finite
> mind of the eternal act of creation in the infinite I AM.[3]

So, for Coleridge, the imagination is part of the image of God in us, a reflection of the divine. It is "a repetition in the finite mind of the eternal act of creation in the infinite I AM."

The purpose of this book is to explore the awe-inspiring consequences of that insight, and to show how there may be an encouragement and, more than that, a wake-up call to Christian artists. How all of us might have a part to play in lifting the veil, removing the film of familiarity, opening our eyes and ears and, most of all our hearts, not only to the "loveliness and wonders of the world before, an inexhaustible treasure" but also to the one through all these things were made and in whom they hold together.

Some years ago, I delivered the three Laing Lectures, at Regent College in Vancouver, under the title "Imagining the Kingdom." In those lectures I focused on how the art of poetry, the art form I understand best, might kindle our imaginations afresh for Christ—how poetry might strengthen and focus our moral and prophetic imagination. In this little book I am re-presenting and expanding those lectures with a new focus, offering them particularly to those who both delight in and enjoy the imaginative arts, and to the artists themselves, to all of you who are stewards of our collective imagination, who by your own shaping and making, continue to create works of imagination to awaken the minds and cleanse the vision of a new generation.

Why Defend the Imagination?

But why should I have to make the case at all? Why does the imagination need defending? To answer these questions, we need briefly to look at the huge changes in the way we think and know, changes in the roles of reasoning on the one hand and intuition on the other, which occurred during the Enlightenment period and came to define the modern era. These changes, which helped to establish the scientific method, and have undoubtedly brought many benefits, did not come without a cost, and the rigorous skepticism which might be appropriate to one sphere of enquiry cast a long shadow over other important areas of human life. As I have argued in my book *Faith, Hope and Poetry*,[4] the Enlightenment ushered in a mistrust and marginalisation of imaginative and poetic vision and a particular suspicion of the ambivalent or multivalent language of poetry. Instead of acknowledging, as many thinkers do now, that *the way we know,* the language through which we know, may be an essential and helpful part of knowledge itself, some philosophers of the Enlightenment thought that image and imagination simply clouded and obscured the pure dry knowledge which they were after. This attitude is often traced back rhetorically to Francis Bacon, who wrote, "For all that concerns ornaments of speech, similitudes, treasury of eloquence, and such like emptinesses, let it be utterly dismissed"[5]—though Bacon himself could not say anything without constantly availing himself of metaphor and symbol, nor can there be any scientific discourse without them.[6]

One of the most telling and influential writings of this period is The Preface to Thomas Sprat's *History of the Royal Society.* Here we see a clear stand against poetry and the poetic imagination as ways of coming at truth, which was to have enormous influence. Sprat urged his readers:

> to separate the knowledge of Nature, from the colours of Rhetoric,
> the devices of Fancy or the delightful deceit of Fables.[7]

The new Philosophers and Scientists had declared war on the imagination and the consequence of that war was a kind of cultural apartheid. The entire realm of "objective" truth was to be the exclusive terrain of *Reason* at its narrowest: analytic, reductive, atomising, and the faculties of *Imagination* and *Intuition,* those very faculties which alone were capable of integrating, synthesising, and making sense of our atomised factual knowledge were relegated to a purely private and "subjective" truth. If it can't be weighed and measured, these men were saying, it's not really there. How prophetic Blake, the great rebel against this division was when he wrote:

> "What," it will be Question'd, "When the Sun rises, do you not see
> a round Disk of fire somewhat like a Guinea?" O no, no, I see an
> Innumerable company of the Heavenly host crying, "Holy, Holy,
> Holy is the Lord God Almighty."[8]

So, we were left torn between an increasingly bleak reductionism which gave us data but no meaning, and an increasingly dislocated and orphaned imaginative and intuitive life crying endlessly for meaning but finding no actual purchase on the facts. This had terrible consequences both on the way we see the world, which came to be seen more and more as an agglomeration of dead stuff to be exploited, and also on the faith. Given this divide, Christians themselves were divided, with some of them driven to a mere literalism which treated the whole vast poem of scripture as though it were some kind of literalistic science manual, and others abandoning any real historical and factual core to the Gospel and just agreeing to treat it as a set of symbols which they could re-invent or re-interpret in any way that suited them. Samuel Taylor Coleridge grasped the problem when, in "The Stateman's Manual," his great lay sermon on the importance of the Bible, he wrote:

> A hunger-bitten and idea-less philosophy naturally produces a starveling and comfortless religion. It is among the miseries of the present age that it recognises no medium, between Literal and Metaphorical. Faith is either to be buried in the dead letter, or its name and honours usurped by a counterfeit product ...[9]

Samuel Taylor Coleridge, an illustration by Daniel Maclise

Lewis as an Example

But we can come closer to our own age for an expression of this dilemma as we feel it now, for C.S. Lewis felt it in in the days of his atheism. Writing of his life as a philosophy tutor in the Oxford of the 1920s, he said:

> The two hemispheres of my mind were in the sharpest contrast. On the one side a many-islanded sea of poetry and myth; on the other a glib and shallow "rationalism." Nearly all that I loved I believed to be imaginary; nearly all that I believed to be real I thought grim and meaningless.[10]

Many of us will resonate with those words, but we have hope! We are living through another of the great shifts in our way of thinking as we come to the end of the Modern Period and there is a chance to heal this split and dislocation. In this book I want to make the case for a recovery and reintegration of the imagination together with the reason as modes of knowing, and further, I want to affirm that the healing of that split, the reconciliation of that division, is to be found in the incarnation, death, and resurrection of Jesus Christ. He comes not only to save us from our sins, but also to heal the tragic fracture in our ways of knowing. In a poem written at the time when Lewis was experiencing this conflict between his reason and imagination, he calls out for a reconciler.

Reason
Set on the soul's acropolis the reason stands
    A virgin arm'd, commercing with celestial light,
And he who sins against her has defiled his own
Virginity: no cleansing makes his garment white;
So clear is reason. But how dark, imagining,
Warm, dark, obscure and infinite, daughter of Night:
Dark is her brow, the beauty of her eyes with sleep
Is loaded, and her pains are long, and her delight.
Tempt not Athene. Wound not in her fertile pains
Demeter, nor rebel against her mother-right.
Oh who will reconcile in me both maid and mother,
Who make in me a concord of the depth and height?
Who make imagination's dim exploring touch
Ever report the same as intellectual sight?
Then could I truly say and not deceive,
Then wholly say that I BELIEVE.[11]

The Transfiguration of Christ, from The Fall and Salvation of Mankind Through the Life and Passion of Christ,
a woodcut by Albrecht Altdorfer

In this poem Lewis represents or embodies reason and imagination, these two ways of knowing, as two goddesses: Athene and Demeter. Lewis equally honours both reason and imagination, seeing them not as blind responses to the environment or even passive faculties but as living powers of the soul. He knows he cannot deny reason but neither can he wound nor rebel against the shaping power of his imagination. He knows that if truth is one, these two ways of approaching truth must be reconciled: but who is their reconciler? And here, of course, we see, with hindsight, how Lewis's powerfully imagined question already carries the intuition of its own answer. We cannot help but hear the echoes of Paul's great prayer in Ephesians:

> For this reason I bow my knees before the Father, from whom every family in heaven and on earth is named, that according to the riches of his glory he may grant you to be strengthened with might through his Spirit in the inner man, and that Christ may dwell in your hearts through faith; that you, being rooted and grounded in love, may have power to comprehend with all the saints what is the breadth and length and height and depth, and to know the love of Christ which surpasses knowledge, that you may be filled with all the fulness of God.[12]

It is Christ, indeed, who reconciles the height and depth, Christ who brings all that is invisible and intuited into the realm of the visible and the known, Christ in whom the Word is made flesh. And in that incarnation, he comes into the World through one who is both maid and mother! And we all know the story of how Lewis found the answer to the question he asks in this poem, strolling on Addison's Walk with Tolkien and Hugo Dyson, how Tolkien showed him that all he loved, imaginatively, intuitively in the great myths of Balder and Adonis, could satisfy his reason and his empirical senses too, and could be found true and reliable in Christ. For in Christ the great *mythos* or story of Death and Resurrection which had haunted the imagination of the poets and story-tellers, was made *history*, and brought into the realm of knowable facts. It was this conversation, as Lewis testifies, that opened the way for him into Christian Faith, and as the two hemispheres of Lewis's mind came together around Christ himself, extraordinary creative power was released in him and Tolkien alike. Coming to Christ, for Lewis, not only changed and deepened the way he understood Christianity but clarified and deepened his whole way of seeing the World, so that later he wrote:

> I believe in Christianity as I believe that the Sun has risen not only
> because I see it but because by it I see everything else.[13]

I had the great privilege of being present at Westminster Abbey in 2013 when Lewis was finally recognised with a plaque in Poet's Corner, and these words about the sunrise were engraved there forever in stone.

It should not surprise us that, in Christ, Lewis found a reconciliation of reason and imagination and therefore found he could trust the imagination as well as the reason as truth-bearing faculty or, as Lewis more precisely put it later, as the organ of meaning:

> Reason is the natural organ of truth; but imagination
> is the organ of meaning.[14]

It is not surprising, because if we understand the incarnation aright, if we know what we mean when we say "the Word was made flesh"—then we will see Christ as the incarnation of God's *meaning* in all things as well as his *love* for all things.

Shakespeare on the Poetic Imagination

I believe that Shakespeare can help us understand that link a little more fully. Here is Shakespeare's famous account of how the poetic imagination actually works:

> The poet's eye, in a fine frenzy rolling,
> Doth glance from heaven to earth, from earth to heaven;
> And, as imagination bodies forth
> The forms of things unknown, the poet's pen
> Turns them to shapes, and gives to airy nothing
> A local habitation and a name.[15]

What is going on here? The first thing to notice is that that the poet starts with observation. But it is active observation, not passive, and it is inclusive of *both* "heaven" and "earth," both visible and invisible. The poet's glance actively takes in both earth and heaven, sees them reciprocally and plays with their relationship. So we have both trajectories, "heaven to earth" and "earth to heaven." Heaven and earth stand for the invisible and the visible worlds, the world we inhabit and seek to comprehend, and the world we can only apprehend imaginatively or by intuition. The artist must pay attention to both.

Some art starts with a "glance to heaven," an intuition of the numinous in the invisible realm of qualities. And having had that glimpse, it seeks to find in the specifics of the world, its materials and quantities, some way of manifesting that apprehended, invisible quality, and so "doth glance from heaven to earth." Other kinds of art start with attention to the particular visible material at hand, the world in front of the artist, the specific physical stuff, the canvas, pigment, clay, or metal, or the words and images with which she makes her art. This art begins with a glance to earth, but then, if it is to be successful art, the glance moves "from earth to heaven" as the artist strives to manifest within the earthly material those transfiguring glimpses of form and quality which can at any moment shimmer through the stuff of this world: the blaze of unconsuming flame that makes a burning bush.

Whichever end of this divine axis between heaven and earth an artist starts from, her only means of seeing and establishing that connection between heaven and earth in her art is imagination. Imagination is at the heart of all artistic making, knowing, and seeing, whether that art is poetic or visual.

And so, having established the field of our imaginative art as always *both* heaven *and* earth, Shakespeare goes on to describe how imagination itself is at work:

Holy Ground, a linocut by Ned Bustard

And as imagination bodies forth
The form of things unknown, the poet's pen
Turns them to shapes . . .

This is astonishing language, especially the juxtaposition of the words "imagination" and "bodies" and the use of "bodies" as a verb!

After the first "stage" of observation or "glancing" where the mind of the artist is receptive, comes stage two: an active imaginative shaping, and giving of form. And that form is expressed as "body," body with all its association of life and growth, of finitude and particularity. The work of imagination is a kind of birthing, a gift of living imaginative form, the making of something that will have its own life and growth and history after the artist has passed on. Because a work of art, in Shakespeare's view, is a living body, it can, in a phrase he uses later in this scene, "grow to something of great constancy."

And what exactly is "bodying forth"? How does it relate to the original artistic challenge, which is the challenge of linking heaven and earth, in the widest senses of those words? Shakespeare answers that question with an image at once of hospitality, particularity, and availability:

> … the poet's pen
> Turns them to shapes, and gives to airy nothing
> A local habitation and a name.

Here we come to the heart of the matter. For most people the "glance" to heaven is just that, a "glance" and no more, a fleeting glimpse, easy to dismiss and overwrite, ignore and explain away. But the artist and poet, by the magical "bodying" power of imagination is able to make a body and build a home for that fleeting glimpse, that "airy nothing" that is always escaping us. The artist makes a home in which that glimpse can root and grow, be found again and again, made knowable and available to us. We have that experience constantly, in returning to poems, paintings, and sculptures which keep giving more than they have, flowing with new life on each visit, because the glimpse which imagination has bodied forth in them has a home in which it can "grow to something of great constancy."

Elsewhere in this same speech Shakespeare pairs the complementary words "apprehend" and "comprehend" alongside the complementary ways of knowing "reason and imagination." He says that imagination "apprehends" more than cool reason ever "comprehends," and again that if imagination "would but comprehend some joy it apprehends some bringer of that joy."

The artist in her imaginative "bodying forth" is building a bridge between apprehension and comprehension. All great art is a bridge with one foot in the world of comprehension, the visible, the earth, and one in the realm of apprehension, the invisible, heaven.

Nativity, an etching by Master IQV

Bodying Forth and Incarnation

However, as I have argued in *Faith, Hope and Poetry,* and elsewhere, this passage in Shakespeare is not simply *literary* language. Its terms and frames of reference *heaven to earth, earth to heaven, bodies forth, form,* and *name* all have a profound *theological* reach. I believe this passage is a kind of commentary and reflection on the account of the incarnation in the prologue to John's Gospel. For in John's prologue heaven itself, the transcendent and otherwise unknowable love, meaning, being, and personhood of God is bodied forth for all of us in the person and in the flesh of Jesus Christ. He *dwells* with us, he takes on *a local habitation and a name.* Furthermore, God's great art of imaginative bodying in Christ indwells and gives meaning to all our own artistic bodying. All art, whether explicitly Christian or not, depends on and participates in that connection made for us by the One who came "from heaven to earth, from earth to heaven," who is and always will be the living bridge between the two.

It is the fact of the incarnation which, itself, underpins and makes possible all the other poetic and imaginative bodyings forth in all the arts of humanity, for we are made in the image of a creator who chose to body himself forth and communicate his love. As Tolkien put it pithily in his poem "Mythopoeia," "We make still by the law by which we were made."[16] It is not simply that we need poetry and the other arts to help us apprehend the mystery of incarnation but that the mystery of incarnation itself is what makes the imaginative arts possible.

To explore this further, let us return for a moment, to the marvellous First Chapter of John's Gospel, and the remarkable encounter between Nathanael with Jesus:

> The next day Jesus decided to go to Galilee. He found Philip and said to him, "Follow me." Now Philip was from Bethsaida, the city of Andrew and Peter. Philip found Nathanael and said to him, "We have found him about whom Moses in the law and also the prophets wrote, Jesus son of Joseph from Nazareth." Nathanael said to him, "Can anything good come out of Nazareth?" Philip said to him, "Come and see." When Jesus saw Nathanael coming toward him, he said of him, "Here is truly an Israelite in whom there is no deceit!" Nathanael asked him, "Where did you get to know me?" Jesus answered, "I saw you under the fig tree before Philip called you." Nathanael replied, "Rabbi, you are the Son of God! You are the King of Israel!" Jesus answered, "Do you believe because I told you that I saw you under the fig tree? You will see greater things than these." And he said to him, "Very truly, I tell you, you will see heaven opened and the angels of God ascending and descending upon the Son of Man."[17]

These verses disclose one of the most mysterious and beautiful moments in the New Testament. As the disciples begin to gather around Jesus, Philip finds Nathanael and says, "We have found him about whom Moses in the law and also the prophets wrote, Jesus son of Joseph from Nazareth." Nathanael's unpromising response is "Can anything good come out of Nazareth?" Nathanael is not alone in having this kind of prejudiced attitude to "other" places and people, but Phillip gives the best possible reply that anyone sharing the mystery of their faith can give: "Come and see." and that "come and see" sets a theme of "seeing" and vision which culminates in the amazing exchange between Nathanael and Jesus that follows.

Before Nathanael has uttered a word Jesus says "Here is truly an Israelite in whom there is no deceit!" and turns the tables of "vision" onto Nathanael himself, and in that moment Nathanael suddenly knows that he is completely known by this man he has never met. "Where did you get to know me?" he asks,

Jacob's Ladder (Heaven), a woodcut by Edward Knippers

and Jesus' reply is again about vision and seeing: "I saw you under the fig tree before Philip called you." Something amazing happens here: Nathanael, who was scoffing at Nazareth a minute before, has a sudden leap of understanding, outpacing reason or teaching, leaping ahead of all the other disciples to an understanding and certainty that even Peter would not attain for another three years, and declares "Rabbi, you are the Son of God! You are the King of Israel!"

An epiphany has taken place, something whole and complete has been disclosed in a single glance, to see and be seen is enough! This is an example in the Gospel of a sudden "awakening," a direct pointing to reality, which some people think is only associated with Buddhism, but here it is in the Gospel! Then Jesus, alluding subtly to Nathanael's mention of Israel, promises that this is just the beginning of a greater epiphany. Nathanael is "truly an Israelite" and Jesus points to the key epiphany in the life of the man Israel, when he was still called Jacob, the epiphany in which he saw the ladder connecting heaven and earth: "Very truly, I tell you, you will see heaven opened and the angels of God ascending and descending upon the Son of Man."

Here is one of those thrilling moments when a mysterious image from the Old Testament finds its fulfillment in the New! The ladder was a prophetic image given in a dream to Jacob of what is to come, and now it has come true! It is as it were, a hidden "I AM saying" preceding the other seven that are given in this Gospel: "I AM Jacob's ladder," Jesus is saying, "the true connection, the true gate of heaven." And in this intimate exchange Nathanael has seen with his waking eyes what his ancestor had seen only veiled in dream and symbol. In my book *Sounding the Seasons* I included a poem reflecting on this mystery:

Nathanael

A fugitive and exile, Jacob slept,
A man of clay, his head upon a stone
And even in his sleep his spirit wept
He lay down lonely and would wake alone.
But in the night he dreamt the Heavens parted
And glimpsed, in glory, as from Heaven's core,
A ladder set for all the broken-hearted
And earth herself becoming Heaven's door.
And when the nameless Angel named him Israel
He kept this gift, whose depth he never knew;
The promise of an end to all our exile,
For now a child of Israel finds it true,
And sees the One who heals the deep heart's aching
As Jacob's dream becomes Nathanael's waking.[18]

What does this mean for us as artists? You will remember how Shakespeare said the artist must "glance from heaven to earth, from earth to heaven," and the artistic imagination must "body forth" the heavenly into the earthly, make the connection and the bridge, but here we see that Christ himself *is* that connection and bridge and if we make our art in and with him, that connection will happen through our art as well. When Jacob woke from his dream he said:

> ... "Surely the LORD is in this place—and I did not know it!" And
> he was afraid, and said, "How awesome is this place! This is none
> other than the house of God, and this is the gate of heaven."[19]

Even his waking vision was still transformed: "How awesome is this place,"
he says, "this is the very gate of heaven." It is the special gift of the imaginative
arts to renew that awe in us, to help us see how any place might suddenly become the very gate of heaven. It is no wonder that William Blake, that prophetic
artist, who along with Coleridge defended the imagination as part of God's image in us, was drawn to the image and meaning of Jacob's ladder, and painted
it beautifully as a wonderful spiral staircase connecting heaven and earth. You
will see the painting on the cover of this book and notice that the angels on
that staircase are not just bringing messages, they are bearing gifts! Two of the
angels who have just descended to where Jacob is sleeping are bearing a platter
of loaves and a jug of wine, the emblems of the sacrament that Jesus would
bring, which is itself a type and emblem of the sacramental quality of all great
art. Beside them, and moving in the heavenward direction, beginning the ascent,
is an angel who bears on her shoulders a little child—the child-like soul of the
true artist, the child within each of us, to whom the kingdom of heaven belongs
and who can still see heaven even when the adult has forgotten how to look!

Jesus' Appeal to the Imagination

From the first moment that he proclaims the Kingdom of God, Jesus appeals to
our imagination where he himself, in his humanity as well as his divinity, becomes
an artist and a poet. He tells the story of the prodigal son, the great tale of a journey
"there and back," of exile and return. In and through that wonderful story, kindled
in our imaginations, and in the imagination of artists and writers down the centuries, Jesus teaches us many many truths: truths about our folly and impatience,
about the way our immature desires can ruin our lives, but truths also about repentance, about return, about what it means to come to yourself and return to
your father's house, and most of all truths about God the Father, and the loving
welcome he still has for us. When Jesus tells the story of the good Samaritan, he is
weaving what might have been, for his first listeners, a most unlikely tale, and yet
it was totally captivating, and at the same time, radically challenging. Expectations
were turned on their head, long-standing prejudices were called out and ques-
tioned, a new way of understanding ourselves and our neighbour, indeed a whole
new understanding of Love was on offer, and all through a "made-up" story! Yet
the maker of that story was Truth himself, and at the deepest level his "fictional"
story, his great parable, was and is true for all time!

The prodigal son seated at the base of a tree among swine . . ., an etching by Pietro Testa

Jesus also appeals to our imagination through the paradoxes of the Gospel, the enigmatic and beautiful signs he gave in his miracles and in those moments when the heavens open and the ordinary is transfigured, seen in an utterly new light. In the gift of faith, and in Christ himself, we glimpse more than we can yet understand, our imagination apprehends more than our reason comprehends. This is not to say that the Gospel is in any way "imaginary" in the dismissive sense of "unreal" or "untrue." On the contrary it is so real and so true that we need every faculty of mind and body, including imagination, to apprehend it. In an age of linear, one-level readings of the word and the world, we need to recover confidence in the baptised imagination as a truth-bearing faculty.

In this book I make the case for an imaginative grasp of faith and an imaginative proclamation of that faith, by considering in turn Christ's appeal to the poetic, the moral, and the prophetic imagination.

Now if it really is the case that the capacity of the imaginative arts to body forth meaning is patterned on and indeed made possible by Christ's incarnation, and that it completes and fulfills more partial ways of knowing, then it should be the case that artists not only help us see God's world more clearly but can also help us to penetrate more deeply into the mystery of Christ, give us a fuller understanding of his mission and meaning. Let us see if that is the case by exploring in the next chapter the ways poets and other artists can usher us further into the mystery of three essential truths about Christ: his Incarnation, Passion, and Resurrection.

NOTES

1   Samuel Taylor Coleridge, *Biographia Literaria*, ed. James Engell and W. Jackson Bate
    (Princeton, NJ: Princeton University Press, 1983), vol. II, p. 7.

2   Coleridge, *Biographica Literaria*, vol. II, p. 6.

3   Coleridge, vol. I, pp. 304–305.

4   Malcolm Guite, *Faith, Hope and Poetry: Theology and the Poetic Imagination*
    (Surrey, UK: Ashgate Publishing, 2008).

5   Francis Bacon, *The Philosophical Works of Francis Bacon*, ed. John M. Robertson
    (London, UK: Routledge, 1905), p. 403.

6   See for example Mary Midgley, Science and Poetry (London, UK: Routledge, 2001).

7   Thomas Sprat, *A History of the Royal Society of London, for the Improving of Natural Knowledge*,
    first edition 1667, taken from the facsimile edited by Cope and Jones. This and subsequent extracts
    from Sprat's influential work can be found on http://newarkwww.rutgers.edu/˜jlynch/Texts/
    sprat.html and on http://www.towson.edu/˜|tinkler/prose/sprat.html.

8   William Blake, "A Vision of the Last Judgment," *Descriptive Catalogue* (1810).

9   Samuel Taylor Coleridge, "The Stateman's Manual," in *Lay Sermons*, ed. R.J. White
    (Princeton, NJ: Princeton University Press, 1972), p. 30.

10 C.S. Lewis, *Surprised by Joy: The Shape of My Early Life* (New York: Harper Collins, 1955),
    pp. 209–210.

11 C.S. Lewis, *The Collected Poems of C.S. Lewis*, ed. Walter Hooper (Fount Paperbacks, 1994), p. 65.

12 Ephesians 3:14–19 (RSV).

13 This famous quote by C.S. Lewis comes from a paper given to The Oxford Socratic Club entitled
    Is Theology Poetry?

14 C.S. Lewis, *Selected Literary Essays*, ed. Walter Hooper (New York: Cambridge University Press,
    1969), p. 265.

15 William Shakespeare, *A Midsummer Night's Dream*, Act V, Scene 1.

16 J.R.R. Tolkien, *Tree and Leaf* (London, UK: HarperCollins Publishers, 1964), pp. 85–90.
    Tolkien wrote this poem in 1931 to C.S. Lewis directly after the famous conversation
    on Addison's Walk.

17 John 1:43–51.

18 Malcolm Guite, "Nathanael," in *Sounding the Seasons: Seventy Sonnets for the Christian Year*
    (London, UK: Canterbury Press, 2012), p. 22.

19 Genesis 28:16–17.

CHRIST
and the
ARTISTIC
IMAGINATION

THE ARTISTIC IMAGINATION can remove the film of familiarity from some of the deepest mysteries of our faith. All my main examples in this chapter will be taken from the art I know best, the art of poetry, but at the end of each one I shall make some suggestions about how other arts—the arts of painting, storytelling, film, or sculpture—might also take us deeper into these same mysteries. We will begin with the central and most distinctive doctrine in Christianity, *The Incarnation*—the all-transforming idea that the Word was made flesh and dwelt among us.

The Incarnation

We have been using Latinate words like *Incarnation* which can be very abstract. We may choose to use a Greek word like *kenosis* ("emptying") or speak of the *Logos* ("Word") becoming *Sarx* ("flesh"), but there is a danger that our language is either abstract and disembodied. For even when we use the word *flesh,* that word is so general that we don't see the intimate particularity of which we are speaking. This is where we need the arts, and in this case poetry. So let's look again at the incarnation through the eyes of Luci Shaw, one of the great lights of contemporary Christian poetry. Here is her poem "Kenosis":

Kenosis

In sleep his infant mouth works in and out.
He is so new, his silk skin has not yet
been roughed by plane and wooden beam
nor, so far, has he had to deal with human doubt.

He is in a dream of nipple found,
of blue-white milk, of curving skin
and, pulsing in his ear, the inner throb
of a warm heart's repeated sound.

His only memories float from fluid space.
So new he has not pounded nails, hung a door
broken bread, felt rebuff, bent to the lash,
wept for the sad heart of the human race.[1]

The poet's capacity to *imagine* the infant Jesus in such vivid detail, far from leading us into the world of the *imaginary*, in the sense of the made-up or not quite real, actually takes us closer to what we mean by both *kenosis* and *incarnation*. Indeed, there is a kind of irony and humility in the title "Kenosis." This poem certainly helps us to understand what it means to say of Christ that

> though he was in the form of God, [he] did not regard equality
> with God as something to be exploited, but emptied himself,
> taking the form of a slave, being born in human likeness.[2]

But after using the word *kenosis* for her title, Shaw engages in her own humble, poetic kenosis: she empties herself of all theological jargon, all abstract technical language and gives us a poem that is so faithful to the flesh that the spirit shines through it.

> In sleep his infant mouth works in and out.
> He is so new, his silk skin has not yet
> been roughed by plane and wooden beam
> nor, so far, has he had to deal with human doubt.

The tiny observation of the infant mouth working in and out, so true to life, says more about the miracle of incarnation than those stiff, hieratic, rather doll-like figures with haloes that we see in so much religious art. Yet she has presented a powerful paradox, simply in the juxtaposition of the words *infant* and *mouth*, for *infans* in Latin means "without speech," so here is the mouth of the

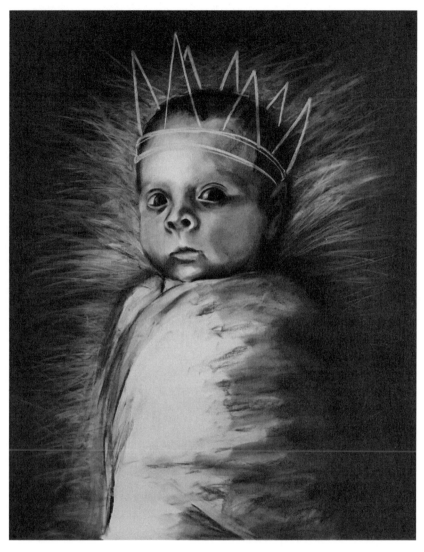

The Vulnerable God, a charcoal drawing by Craig Hawkins

Word, unable to speak a word. Here is kenosis indeed: the one who speaks all things into being empties and humbles himself until he can only receive. And yet by introducing the poetic device of the "not yet," she is able with two simple images of the plane and the wooden beam to foreshadow for us that Passion and self-offering, of which the incarnation was the beginning, that kenosis which would be obedient unto death. And in the last line of this first verse she takes this further, for the descent is not simply into humanity but into humanity's experience of lostness, disconnection, and doubt. Even in that word "doubt"

Incarnate, a drawing by Stephen Crotts

we hear, as it were, the backward travelling echo of the cry of dereliction from
the Cross.

And then, in the beautiful second verse her poetry empties us out of our
adult selves and draws us into his vivid experience of infancy and ours.

> He is in a dream of nipple found,
> of blue-white milk, of curving skin
> and, pulsing in his ear, the inner throb
> of a warm heart's repeated sound.

And in her final verse, whose few lines take us image by image through his
life from an apprenticeship to Joseph, through communion to the passion, she
leaves us not only with our compassion for him, which we might have thought

was the subject of the poem, but also with his compassion for us as he weeps weeps "for the sad heart of the human race."

Of course, there are many other art forms as well as poetry, which can help us understand what "kenosis" and incarnation really mean. But there may be some traditions in art and iconography which were helpful once but are less helpful to us now. Consider the many traditional paintings of the Virgin and Child: some of these are so keen to emphasise the glory of the moment and the holiness of Mary that they show her resplendent in rich robes, comfortable in the portico of a Renaissance building. Even if they allow the setting to be a stable they clean the stable up and fill it was so many finely clad angels that we lose the sense of the dirt, squalor, and danger into which Christ chose to be born. Also some of the artists were so keen to stress the kingship of Christ, even in his infancy, that instead of the tiny babe "in a dream of nipple found, of blue-white milk," they show a stiff little figure gazing out with preternatural wisdom and already giving a full episcopal blessing. But not always: there is for example *The Newborn Christ,* a very beautiful painting by Georges de la Tour from the mid-seventeenth century. Here there is a strong and yet tender realism. Christ is painted very much as a tiny new-born infant, his eyes closed in blissful sleep, that delicate, new-baby softness to his skin as he is held so carefully, as a fragile and precious bundle by Mary. And yet, just by the reverent demeanour of the two female figures, the gesture at once of blessing and worship from Elizabeth, and by the extraordinary light which seems to flow from as much as to rest upon Christ, the artist has suggested his divinity shining in and through his humanity.

The Passion

Let us turn now from Christ's incarnation to his Passion, to the atonement, to what he achieved for us and disclosed to us in his suffering and death. Again we have no shortage of theological language available, and the approach of rational and systematic theology has given us many helpful ideas and theories. I do not deny that they are useful, but here I am asking whether the poetic imagination can complement that knowledge, can offer us some apprehensions that begin just where comprehension has found its limit. The poem I have chosen to probe this mystery is George Herbert's "The Agony" which, as it happens, begins with this very question of what we think we already know, and how turning to Christ can deepen and indeed radically transform that knowledge:

The Agony

    Philosophers have measur'd mountains,
Fathom'd the depths of seas, of states and kings;
Walk'd with a staff to heav'n and traced fountains:
    But there are two vast, spacious things,
The which to measure it doth more behove;
Yet few there are that sound them,—Sin and Love.

    Who would know Sin, let him repair
Unto Mount Olivet; there shall he see
A Man so wrung with pains, that all His hair,
    His skin, His garments bloody be.
Sin is that press and vice, which forceth pain
To hunt his cruel food through ev'ry vein.

    Who knows not Love, let him assay
And taste that juice which, on the cross, a pike
Did set again abroach; then let him say
    If ever he did taste the like,
Love is that liquor sweet and most divine,
Which my God feels as blood, but I as wine.[3]

In "The Agony," Herbert shows us how the Passion of Christ, from his agony in the garden to the shedding of his blood on the cross, helps us entirely to re-configure and renew our understanding first of sin, as it presses, squeezes, and crushes our humanity, and then of the love that meets with sin and redeems it.

The first three lines of this poem sum up our apparently impressive but actually empty ways of knowing. From there Herbert turns to deal with what is missing from the empty heart of such merely outer knowledge:

    … two vast spacious things
The which to measure it doth more behove;
Yet few there are that sound them,—Sin and Love.

"Sin and Love." How are we to know these things? Our own age would make the knowledge purely personal and self-contained—a little dip into what we think we know about our private psychology. Herbert has a quite different approach.

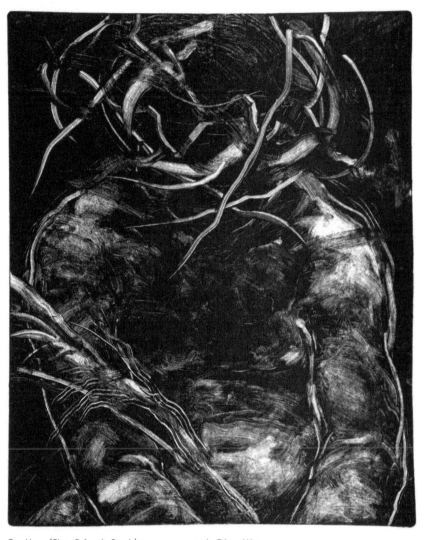

Ecce Homo (Christ Before the People), a monotype print by Edward Knippers

First of all he asks us to know *both* Sin *and* Love, to know them *together*, to know that Sin is what it is because it assaults and denies Love, and that Love is what it is precisely because it answers, heals, and redeems the very sin that assaults it. But the contemporary church, in its different branches, seems to me to have separated and split apart two kinds of knowing which should be mutually enfolded. So on one block in town you can find a church that knows all about sin, that preaches constantly on our total depravity and how the wrath of God is revealed against all sin and how hell is opening wide its jaws for us, but that seems to have very little understanding of love. The Love that bears all things, the Love that hopes all things, the Love that welcomes us as sinners and asks us to welcome precisely those people we are inclined to condemn—that Love seems to be absent. And of course just round the same block you can find another church that knows all about love and is full of affirmation, inclusion, and indeed is ready to affirm anything and everything in such an indiscriminate way as to make you think that we live in an unfallen world, that everything is absolutely fine—if we just affirm everything then nobody is ever actually guilty of anything. Now we might have our own view on which side of that divide it is better to err, but I think we can recognise that there is something so partial, so incomplete as to be false in each of those approaches taken by themselves.

But Herbert draws our attention to *both*, not just one: *two* vast and spacious things. He has the courage to see sin for what it is because he also knows love, and his love is not some bland or blind wishful thinking because he also knows sin. It is the vision of Christ in Gethsemane and on the cross, which allows him to see both. Our only hope of really knowing ourselves, says Herbert, is to look for a light beyond ourselves and come to know God, for he himself knows us better than we can know ourselves, so that one day we can know fully, even as we have been fully known.[4]

For Herbert, the only way we know God, the only possible place and person in which we can meet him is Christ. In Christ God meets us in our humanity. It is from the passion of Christ that we learn both who God is and who we are. Let's hear again that second stanza:

> Who would know Sin, let him repair
> Unto Mount Olivet; there shall he see
> A Man so wrung with pains, that all His hair,
> His skin, His garments bloody be.
> Sin is that press and vice, which forceth pain
> To hunt his cruel food through ev'ry vein.

In this verse, with its vivid images of Christ's agony in the garden, Herbert is saying that Christ's agony is also an image of our inner condition; it is at one and the same time an image both of what Sin does to a person and an image of God's loving response, which bears and transforms the sheer weight of sin. For Herbert the very fact that Jesus had to endure such agony in order to deliver us from "that press and vice" reveals how serious a thing sin is.

The image of Christ crushed in the "press and vice" is profound because it expresses not only the pain and pressure of Gethsemane, which means "Olive Press," squeezing the very blood to the surface of Christ's body, but also because

Christ in the Wine Press, an engraving by Hieronymus Wierix

it alludes to the rich biblical symbolism of the wine press. The wine press is a symbol both of wrath and of generosity. There is the wine press of wrath from the Old Testament:

I have trodden the winepress alone...
For I will tread them in mine anger,
and trample them in my fury;
and their blood shall be sprinkled upon my garments,
and I will stain all my raiment.[5]

But this image of a wrathful God, coming covered in the blood of those upon whom he has taken just vengeance, was daringly and paradoxically applied to Christ by the Church Fathers, both to suggest that in making atonement it is his own blood which Christ spills instead of ours, and also to make a symbolically profound reversal of the Old Testament metaphor. In Isaiah the wine crushed from the grapes symbolizes blood; in the radical Christian reading of that passage, the garments dipped in blood presage Christ's gift of his own blood as wine. And all this symbolic background is focused, and *expressed* (in every sense of that term) in the concentrated imagery of the poem; the sign of wrath becomes the sign of redemption as "Sin" is transmuted by "Love" and from this "press" flows the wine which will be the life of the communicant church. So in his third and final stanza Herbert moves from the contemplation in Christ of "sin" to contemplation in Christ of that "love" which redeems sin:

Who knows not Love, let him assay
And taste that juice which, on the cross, a pike
Did set again abroach; then let him say
    If ever he did taste the like,
Love is that liquor sweet and most divine,
Which my God feels as blood, but I as wine.

He who trod the winepress alone becomes the cask of wine to be pierced, "set abroach," opened, to refresh his people. It is an astonishing and daring metaphor to make the moment the soldier's pike pierces Christ's heart on the cross—a vision of the 'setting abroach' of a wine cask.

Who knows not Love, let him assay
And taste that juice which, on the cross, a pike
Did set again abroach;'

The poem finishes with an expression of the mystery of incarnation and sacrament which is God's divine exchange and intercommunion offered to man on the cross:

Love is that liquor sweet and most divine,
Which my God feels as blood, but I as wine.

In some ways that final couplet offers an epitome of the claims I want to make for poetry. Think of all the ink, and indeed blood, that has been spilt by the church in its endless arguments attempting to define rationally the exact way in which Christ is present to us in communion, of how Aquinas borrowed the language of "substance" and "accident" from Aristotle's *Physics* to create the term "transubstantiation," how the reformers argued instead for trans-significa-tion, how time and again the mystery was, in Edwin Muir's memorable phrase, "impaled and bent / into an ideological argument"[6] and then comes Herbert and in two lines of poetry he says something which is adequate to everyone's experience, Catholic and Protestant alike, something that takes us to the heart of the whole atonement, whatever model you use, takes us straight to Love himself.

We have used the example of poetry, but once more we can think of how many of the other arts remove the film of familiarity and move us more deeply into the mystery of the passion. In the realm of painting one thinks of Matthias Grünewald's harrowing depiction of the Crucifixion from the *Isenheim Altarpiece*. The closer you look, the more you see Christ's body torn and scarred and pitted with thorns and wounds. The crushing weight of pain and sorrow that

Center panel of *The Isenheim Altarpiece*, painted by Matthias Grünewald

bears down on all of fallen humanity seems to be the very force that wrenches his head downwards as his agonised face looks towards the earth, and yet his outstretched arms and upraised hands, even as the fingers writhe in pain, seem to lift the whole earth back up to God in prayer. Despite the stock Christian symbols of the passion's meaning—the two vessels for communion; John the Baptist with the sacrificial lamb at his feet, pointing to Christ as the true lamb of God— it is not the iconography but the sheer humanity of this depiction of undeserved pain that speaks through the eye to the heart of the beholder.

A modern equivalent of Grünewald's approach might be the film *The Passion of Christ*,[7] which follows him in forcing upon us the sheer gruesome and physical detail of flogging and crucifixion. For some filmgoers this was almost too much, but unless we grasp that the experience of crucifixion itself was more than too much we will not penetrate to the heart of the mystery. Grünewald's approach is a deliberate counterpoint to earlier depictions of the Crucifixion which show Christ reigning from the cross, somehow still in full control, with angels in attendance, holding Chalice to the wounds from which the sacraments will flow. This represents another side of the truth, but we need both kinds of art if we are to catch something more of this multifaceted mystery.

Yet another way that the artistic imagination can approach and illuminate the meaning of the passion is to take it out of its original setting and reimagine it in our own. I had some personal experience of this, which was also an experience of the wonderful way in which one piece of art begets and generates another, of the way in which artists kindle one another's imagination as well as that of their audience. During the Holy Week and Easter of our first lockdown in England, when we once more contemplated the all-transforming mystery of the passion and resurrection of Christ, but had to do so outside our locked churches, I wrote a poem called "Easter 2020" in which I imagined Christ at one with, in complete solidarity with, those suffering from Covid in hospitals and those ministering to them, experiencing his own passion in and through them and lending them his strength. The final verse of that poem went like this:

> On Thursday we applauded, for he came
> And served us in a thousand names and faces
> Mopping our sickroom floors and catching traces
> Of that *corona* which was death to him:
> Good Friday happened in a thousand places
> Where Jesus held the helpless, died with them
> That they might share his Easter in their need,
> Now they are risen with him, risen indeed.[8]

This poem was seen by the artist Bruce Herman and it moved him to make a new work: *Good Friday Happened in a Thousand Places* (see the back cover of this book), a collage in which he reimagined and remade *Second Adam*, one of his own existing and powerful paintings of the passion. But for this new work, in the space where in a traditional painting there might have been angels hovering above Christ on the cross or flying in the space beside him, Bruce Herman placed images of contemporary nurses in their full PPE (personal protective equipment) moving in procession towards the Christ figure. It was a powerful artistic statement, not least because as all art should do, it de-sentimentalised and re-vivified a cliché, for we often speak of nurses as angels, even as ministering angels. But the angels in this painting are strong, compassionate, courageous, like the Christ to whom they are moving. Bruce Herman's work takes the passion out of an ethereal art world and puts it back where it belongs in the midst of everyday life and yet it does so without losing any of its meaning or glory. Indeed, there are hints and glints of iconic gold showing through the blue of the paint, and yet resting as it were on such a column of gold is the everyday cardboard box containing the nurses' PPE. In some ways, this new work lifted a veil not only from the passion but from my own poem too.[9]

The Resurrection

Let us turn finally, in this exploration of how the poetic imagination clarifies, or perhaps intensifies our vision both of Christ and the world he loves, to the mystery of his glorious resurrection, and therefore of the new creation which that resurrection initiates. Now here I'm going to do something rather unexpected, but I hope I can justify it. Rather than take you to a poem directly about the resurrection, I am going to discuss poetry about the Transfiguration, that glimpse of Christ in glory vouchsafed to the disciples just before they had to turn their faces towards Jerusalem and go with him to see him suffer. I remember reading a

Resurrection, an alabaster sculpture by an anonymous English sculptor, c. 1450.

The Transfiguration, ink and gouache on scratchboard by Tanja Butler

commentary once, which described the Transfiguration as "a misplaced resurrection narrative." After I had recovered from my initial irritation with this
high-handed commentator who seemed to think he could tick St. Luke off for
making a slight mistake with his cutting and pasting, I realized that although
the accounts of the Transfiguration in the Gospels are certainly not misplaced,

they are in a very profound sense "resurrection narratives." That is to say, they are glimpses vouchsafed even now, whilst we walk through the valley of the shadow of death, of that great light, that great sun-rising which begins the new creation. And, strictly speaking, this is true of the Resurrection itself, for Christ rises as "the first fruits of the new creation." If we are to understand the glimpse of Christ in his Transfiguration in this way, as a sign of resurrection, something which the living presence of Moses and Elijah also suggest, then it is definitely not misplaced. A mountain-top moment of clear vision is granted to the disciples before they descend into the confusing and sometimes blinding fog of events that lead to the apparent defeat of the Crucifixion. In so far as the Transfiguration clarifies vision, and is itself a visionary experience, then in some sense it corresponds with the role of poetry and the poetic imagination in the Christian life: for poetry, says Coleridge, removes the film of familiarity and restores our missing sense of wonder.

The Scottish twentieth-century mystical poet Edwin Muir wrote a long and interesting poem about the Transfiguration, which suggests that to see Christ's Transfiguration is to be transfigured yourself, and that Transfiguration restores to you a vision of the world, *sub specie aeternitatis*, as God sees it. To be present at the Transfiguration was not to have climbed away from the world, but to have come suddenly on its holy and sacred source "as fresh and pure as water from a well." The poem opens like this:

> So from the ground we felt that virtue branch
> Through all our veins till we were whole, our wrists
> As fresh and pure as water from a well,[10]

These lines draw beautifully on echoes of the Old Testament as they have been woven into liturgy. The *Beatus Vir* that opens the Psalms and says of the virtuous man:

> And he shall be like a tree planted by the rivers of water,
> that bringeth forth his fruit in his season;
> His leaf also shall not wither;
> And whatsoever he doeth shall prosper.[11]

And Jeremiah's anticipatory beatitude:

> Blessed is the man that trusteth in the LORD, and whose hope the
> LORD is. For he shall be as a tree planted by the waters, and that
> spreadeth out her roots by the river, and shall not see when heat

cometh, but her leaf shall be green; and shall not be careful in the
year of drought, neither shall cease from yielding fruit.[12]

And there is a memory too, drawn from the well of the Prophet Isaiah:

Therefore with joy shall ye draw water
out of the wells of salvation.[13]

So in the opening of Muir's poem what he calls "that virtue" rises out of deep
roots, rises as pure water, to cleanse and renew the disciples from within, as the
next two lines of the poem show:

Our hands made new to handle holy things,
The source of all our seeing rinsed and cleansed[14]

These lines are really the key to the whole poem, and indeed, a summary of
what poetry has to offer: a *rinsing and cleansing* of vision so that we see whole
and clear again, not just with the reductive, myopic vision of our habitual materialism. This is what Coleridge was speaking of in a passage we have already
cited when in his *Biographia Literaria* he described what he and Wordsworth
hoped to achieve in their joint book *Lyrical Ballads.* For them, the poetic imagination is not about lulling us, distracting us, or compensating with fantasy for
the grim reality of the world, but rather:

awakening the mind's attention from the lethargy of custom, and
directing it to the loveliness and the wonders of the world before
us; an inexhaustible treasure, but for which in consequence of the
film of familiarity and selfish solicitude we have eyes, yet see not,
ears that hear not, and hearts that neither feel nor understand.[15]

I think both Coleridge's comments and Edwin Muir's poem were in my mind
when I came to compose my own poem on the Transfiguration. I loved Muir's
idea that in seeing Christ transfigured the disciples had had the very sources of
their seeing "rinsed and cleansed," and that, therefore, it was not only Christ, but
the whole of creation which would begin to be transfigured. Having seen Christ
unveiled they would begin to glimpse the glory behind the veil everywhere. But
there was something in Edwin Muir's long poem with which I wish to take issue:
towards the end of his poem, as he imagines the disciples perceiving "the radiant kingdom" everywhere, he also imagines a kind of undoing or unmaking of
the cross as Christ returns whole:

Then he will come, Christ the uncrucified
Christ the discrucified, his death undone,
His agony unmade his cross dismantled—[16]

I delight in the hope the poet offers, of that time "when triune is ripe and Christ will come again to make all things new." I applaud the way he sees that second coming as not simply a redemption of mankind *from* the world, but a re-making of the world *in* and *with* mankind. That promise is Good News, as Paul also knew, for nature as well as humanity: "For the creation waits with eager longing for the revealing of the children of God."[17]

But amidst my delight in Muir's poem, I also feel a strange sharp shock that this beloved poet has somehow missed a central truth, indeed the heart of the Gospel. It is understandable that he wants to make everything right, to make everything better, but he seems to think that the only way to do this is to un-do and un-say all the hurts, to run time backwards and start again as though the giant agony of the world and the Crucifixion itself, in which God entered that agony,

Detail from *Golgotha*, a woodcut by Robert Hodgell

The Transfiguration with Christ flanked by two saints and with the Apostles below, an engraving by Cherubino Alberti

had never happened. And so he imagines a Christ, uncrucified, discrucified, his death undone, "his agony unmade." He seems to believe that just as for Judas, so for all of us, the journey into redemption must be a nostalgic journey backwards to Eden and not an adventurous journey forwards to the City of God, that City where the lamb who was slain is on the throne.

He is wrong! For a Christian there can never be a Christ discrucified, for it is Christ crucified who is "the power of God and the wisdom of God."[18] There is no going back, there is no unmaking, and we know this for ourselves. Terrible as our own sufferings may have been, we cannot undo them, and if we have borne them, and know that Christ bears them with us, then we also know that he has been making and shaping us into the people we are, the people he loves, precisely through those experiences.

So my poem on the Transfiguration in some sense takes its cue from Edwin Muir, in others it pushes back. For although my poem is about the Transfiguration and through the Transfiguration the promise of resurrection, the poem is actually set on Good Friday, for the narrator is standing at the foot of the cross looking at the blackened sky and the darkened scars, but looking at them in the light of what he can remember of the Transfiguration, so that that light, even if only remembered can sustain him through this darkness.

> Transfiguration
> For that one moment, "in and out of time,"
> On that one mountain where all moments meet,
> The daily veil that covers the sublime
> In darkling glass fell dazzled at his feet.
> There were no angels full of eyes and wings
> Just living glory full of truth and grace.
> The Love that dances at the heart of things
> Shone out upon us from a human face
> And to that light the light in us leaped up,
> We felt it quicken somewhere deep within,
> A sudden blaze of long-extinguished hope
> Trembled and tingled through the tender skin.
> Nor can this blackened sky, this darkened scar
> Eclipse that glimpse of how things really are.[19]

My line "On that one mountain where all moments meet," was inspired by the presence of Christ on the mountain with Moses and Elijah, both of whom in their own time and place had mountain-top experiences of transfigured illumination, both of whom saw God in some ineffable way. I wondered if their

Moses Before the Burning Bush, an engraving by Claude Mellan

appearance in the presence of Christ on this mountain top was not a repetition of that first experience or a re-visiting of this World by these Old Testament figures, who represent between them the Law and the Prophets, but rather that the disciples were witnessing the truth that in the light of heaven, in heaven's time as it were, those three separate moments: Moses' on his mountain in his time, Elijah in his, and Christ in this Gospel moment were all one moment! If Moses and Elijah saw the face of God in a mystery then it could be none other than the face of Christ. Indeed, there is a direct symbolic and imaginative link between Moses' first vision of God in the burning bush and this vision of Christ. As many Christian commentators from Augustine even down as far as Calvin have observed, just as the bush was completely illuminated by the fire of God's holy presence, and yet not consumed, every leaf still as green and growing and biologically intact as ever, so in Christ human and divine nature are united and mutually illuminated, but neither overwhelms nor eradicates the other. Christ is fully divine, "in him all the fullness of God was pleased to dwell,"[20] and yet he was also full human from first to last, crying as a human baby in the manger and dying in human agony on the cross. Of course, it is speaking from the burning bush that God makes the promise only completely fulfilled in Christ: "and I have come down to deliver them."[21]

Both the burning bush and the Transfiguration are essential paradigms for the Christian artist. The artist must completely respect the earthly and human integrity of the material they work with: they are not to obscure or overwrite God's good earth with theological slogans however pious, the bush must still be a bush deeply rooted in the earth. And yet, in the handling and imagination of a Christian artist it must become what R.S. Thomas called the "lit bush."[22] It must draw us as the burning bush drew Moses, to turn aside to take off our shoes from our feet and to see with a gasp of wonder that the ordinary has been transfigured, that the veil has been lifted and the glory of God's presence has been shining through.

We touched in the opening chapter on the prologue to John's Gospel. Let us turn again to the great account of the incarnation. Having said that "the Word was made flesh, and dwelt among us," John goes on to say "and we seen his glory, the glory as of the only begotten of the Father, full of grace and truth."[23] It might be worth asking what experience the prologue of John is referring to here. Whoever was the compiler, it is tempting to see in that phrase an authentic eyewitness narrative since it was Peter, James, and John who witnessed the Transfiguration on the Mountain. I am sure that is indeed an element of what John meant by "beholding the glory" but only one element. For John sees the glory equally at the dark moment of Jesus' betrayal and his willingness to be betrayed as he does on the mountain top. It is just after Judas leaves to betray Jesus that we are told "it was night" and Jesus says "Now the son of man has been glorified":

> So, after receiving the piece of bread, he immediately went out.
> And it was night. When he had gone out, Jesus said, "Now the Son
> of Man has been glorified, and God has been glorified in him."[24]

So John could never have spoken as Muir did of *"the uncrucified / Christ the discrucified, his death undone / his agony unmade."* We do not reveal or restore Christ's glory by dismantling the cross, but rather by seeing the glory of love shining from those wounds even as the nails are driven in. And, of course, it is John's Gospel that gives us the poignant moment when the risen Christ invites Thomas, the Apostle, to touch his wounds. Our great hymn writers, themselves poets, were right when they gave us lines to sing like "rich wounds yet visible above / in beauty glorified."[25] Edwin Muir was right to hope that "he will come again" but Charles Wesley had an even deeper insight when he wrote "with what rapture, with what rapture, gaze we on those glorious scars."[26]

Christ's Descent into Hell, is one of Albrecht Dürer's depictions of the harrowing of hell.

I have been making the case in this chapter for what Seamus Heaney calls *The Redress of Poetry*,[27] the case that poetry redresses an imbalance in our understanding, that when we seek to enter into the mystery of our faith we must call the poets to the table as well as the theologians. But here I also wish to acknowledge that the imbalance can sometimes work both ways, to acknowledge that if the theologians need the poets, then the poets also need the theologians, that the imagination must come, in its own way, to be baptised and that baptism is part of what it means to have the source of all our seeing rinsed and cleansed.

In reflecting on how these glimpses of transfiguration shadow or show forth the promise of the resurrection, not just Christ's resurrection but the resurrection in Christ that is coming to all of us, and to nature as a whole, I have drawn on my own art, the art of poetry. But it is worth asking how the other arts might help us in glimpsing this Transfiguration, how they have done so in the past and how they might do so in the future. There is a strong tradition in Orthodox iconography of depicting the resurrection not as a solitary private event for Christ but as the harbinger and, indeed, the enabler of our resurrection. So Christ is depicted standing on the broken wood of the Cross and reaching out with both hands to pull Adam and Eve from their graves, and with them the Patriarchs and the Prophets: "all whom he has found and liberated when he harrowed hell."

This is the supreme task of Christian art, not simply to represent the biblical events in their original context, at a distance from us, "out there and back then," but to show them in our context, in the midst of our doubts and difficulties, to show them happening "in here and right now."

In the next chapter I want to explore what it might mean to return to the teachings of Jesus, to his parables and paradoxes, and especially to his teaching about Love and the Kingdom, with the sources of all our seeing rinsed and cleansed, our imaginations baptized, and poetry as our companion in hearing the Gospel afresh.

NOTES

1   Luci Shaw, "Kenosis," in *Harvesting Fog* (Montrose, CO: Pinyon Publishing, 2010), p. 53.

2   Philippians 2:6–7.

3   George Herbert, "The Agony," in *The Temple* (1633).

4   1 Corinthians 13:12.

5   Isaiah 63:3 (KJV, which George Herbert would have used).

6   Edwin Muir, "The Incarnate One," first published in *One Foot in Eden* (1956) and included
     in *Collected Poems* 1921–1958 (London, UK: Faber and Faber, 1960), p. 228.

7   *The Passion of the Christ,* produced and directed by Mel Gibson (Santa Monica, CA:
     Icon Productions, 2004).

8   This poem will be included in one of my forthcoming collections, but has already been
     included in N.T. Wright's book *God and the Pandemic: A Christian Reflection on the
     Coronavirus and Its Aftermath* (Grand Rapids, MI: Zondervan, 2020).

9   This poem and the painting it inspired can be accessed at https://malcolmguite.wordpress.
     com/2020/04/12/easter-2020-a-new-poem/.

10   Edwin Muir, "The Transfiguration," first published in *The Labyrinth* (1949) and included in
     Collected Poems 1921–1958 (London, UK: Faber and Faber, 1960), p. 198.

11   Psalm 1:3 (KJV, as used by Edwin Muir).

12   Jeremiah 17:7–8 (KJV).

13   Isaiah 12:3 (KJV).

14   Muir, "The Transfiguration," p. 198.

15   Samuel Taylor Coleridge, *Biographia Literaria,* ed. James Engell and W. Jackson Bate
     (Princeton, NJ: Princeton University Press, 1983), vol. II, p. 7.

16   Muir, "The Transfiguration," p. 198.

17   Romans 8:19.

18   1 Corinthians 1:24

19   Malcolm Guite, "Transfiguration," in *Sounding the Seasons: Seventy Sonnets for the
     Christian Year* (London, UK: Canterbury Press, 2012), p. 56.

20   Colossians 1:19.

21   Exodus 3:8.

22   R.S. Thomas, extract from "The Bright Field," in *Collected Poems* 1945–1990
     (London, UK: Phoenix, 2000).

23   John 1:14 (KJV).

24   John 13:30–31.

25   Matthew Bridges, "Crown Him with Many Crowns," hymnary.org, accessed May 19, 2021,
     https://hymnary.org/text/crown_him_with_many_crowns

26   Charles Wesley, John Cennick, and Martin Madan, "Lo, He comes With Clouds Descending,"
     hymnary.org, accessed May 4, 2021, https://hymnary.org/hymn/LW1982/15.

27   Seamus Heaney, *The Redress of Poetry* (New York: Farrar, Straus and Giroux, 1995).

CHRIST
and the
MORAL
IMAGINATION

SO FAR WE HAVE SEEN how the incarnation of the *Logos*, that turning point in the story of the cosmos, in which the Word became flesh and the creator entered his creation, was itself a healing and reconciliation of the false split between reason and imagination; comprehension and apprehension; history and myth. Furthermore, we saw that there was a deep parallel between the activity of the poetic imagination at its best, "bodying forth the form of things unknown," in Shakespeare's memorable phrase, and the incarnation itself. And I suggested that, perhaps, it was God's once-and-for all bodying forth in Christ, which underpins and makes possible our own poetic and artistic embodying of meaning.

Parables and Parallels

In this chapter we are going to move from an imaginative apprehension of Christ himself, to focus particularly on Christ's teaching, on the way Jesus appeals to our imagination in his parables, the way he invites us not only to see the beautiful appearances of nature but also to read them imaginatively, to read them as symbols, as a kind of language, so that he can teach us the invisible through the visible. But I want to start by noticing something we all take for granted: that there should be any *parallels* to make up a *parable*, that there should be any correspondence between the outward unfolding of nature and the inner workings of our minds.

If we were to believe the bleak, reductive, and exclusively materialist account of ourselves as a set of survival and defense mechanisms, an unintended series of biochemical reactions, whose sheer complexity has accidentally thrown up our consciousness as a kind of isolated epiphenomenon, then we should scarcely expect there to be any real correspondence between the accidental inner life of our mind and all the supposedly mindless processes of nature going on "out there." We might expect to be aware of a tree so as not to bump into it, or even so as to hide in it, but we should scarcely expect that a tree with its roots and branches should so perfectly express and embody for us the pattern of thought itself, the pattern of history, the nature of organisations and even the inner spiritual life of a person who is "like a tree planted by the waters and bringing forth fruit in due season."[1] There might be good evolutionary reasons for our observing the cycles of sowing and growth in nature, and for our ability to control those processes a little, by ploughing furrows and planting seeds, but the mechanistic and reductive view would scarcely lead us to the actual experience we have: that in letting a seed fall from our hands and be covered in earth, and waiting for its first fruits to rise, we should find a perfect outer emblem for a whole series of inward experiences of loss and letting go that lead to new fruition, let alone that we should find in that cycle of supposedly indifferent and purposeless nature a parable of death and resurrection that whispers a great hope. On the other

Lady with the Rooks, a wood engraving by Edward Calvert

hand, if the Christian assertion is true that all things were created in the *Logos:* in mind, order, and meaning, and that that same *Logos* is also the inner light of every human mind, the light who lightens everyone who comes into the world, then such rich and fruitful parallels between the inner life of the mind and the outer life nature are precisely what we should expect to find! If we were further to assert that this same *Logos,* through whom all of nature was made and who lights every human mind, actually came into the world as a human being, not only to save, but also to teach us, then we would pay special attention to the way in which he himself used the language of the outer world—the seeds, the trees, the birds of the air, and the flowers of the field—to express the life of the spirit. For here, we would have the privilege of meeting and listening to meaning itself or rather we should say, meaning Himself. The author of the cosmos, this great work in which we find ourselves, would be reading to us, and interpreting for us, the poem of his own creation. And that I think is precisely what is happening when we sit at the feet of Jesus and hear him teaching in parables.

We have already had occasion to quote Coleridge a couple of times, and it was Coleridge above all who grasped that the human imagination works in some sense *with* the *Logos,* the divine imagination, which created what Coleridge called:

> The lovely shapes and sounds intelligible
> Of that eternal language, which thy God
> Utters, who from eternity doth teach
> Himself in all, and all things in himself.
> Great universal Teacher! he shall mould
> Thy spirit, and by giving make it ask.[2]

But Coleridge went even further than that, and before we turn to what that "great universal Teacher" actually taught us through the language of nature, when he walked with us in human form, let us return to Coleridge's theological- ly resonant definition of the imagination from the *Biographia Literaria*, as think it will inform and underpin all I have to say in this book:

> The IMAGINATION then I consider either as primary, or secondary. The primary IMAGINATION I hold to be the living Power and prime Agent of all human Perception, as a repetition in the finite mind of the eternal act of creation in the infinite I AM. The secondary I consider as an echo of the former, co-existing with the conscious will, yet still as identical with the primary in the *kind* of its agency, and differing only in *degree,* and in the mode of its operation.[3]

The Sixth Day: The Creation of Animals, Adam and Eve from the Creation of the World, an engraving by Johann Sadeler I

So there are two things for us to note especially here: the first is that Coleridge sees that there is a creative or imaginative element, even agency, in *all perception*—in other words there is already a deep imaginative shaping in the way we see the world. But this does not mean that we should despair with Kant and conclude that we don't see things truly, for the second point that Coleridge makes is that this beautiful, human imaginative shaping of the way we perceive the world is, itself, part of what it means to be made in the image of God. It is, indeed, the work of the *Logos* within us; it is "a repetition in the finite mind of the eternal act of creation in the infinite I AM."[4]

The word *eternal* here is very important. The act of creation is not something that happened *in* time, as though time were already there when creation "began," for time itself is a created thing. As Augustine remarked "God did not make the world with time but in time." This means that all moments in time including the one we are in now, just as much as the moment of the big bang, are all equally close to God's "eternal act of creation." What Coleridge is saying, I think, is that at every moment in which we are conscious and perceive God's world, God is *in that same moment* creating it in and through the *Logos*. And he is inviting us actively to perceive and know his creation through that same *Logos* within us, constantly inviting our finite minds to echo his eternal act in every moment of perception. And because the *Logos* is himself *meaning*, then the more we bring our imagination consciously to Christ and allow it to be baptised, the more we perceive all things in and through Christ, the more even the most ordinary things are transfigured and glimmer into symbol. They become "the shapes and sounds intelligible" of an "eternal language."[5]

It is in that light, and with that understanding, that I want us to turn now to Christ as he teaches us in parables, in the language of that creation which he is, even now, uttering into being.

The Parable of the Grain of Wheat

Let us begin with one of the simplest and yet most central of all Christ's teachings and see how it unfolds for us, if we allow the imagination that Christ has given and arouses to be the prime agent of our perception:

> Jesus answered them, "The hour has come for the Son of Man to be glorified. Very truly, I tell you, unless a grain of wheat falls into the earth and dies, it remains just a single grain; but if it dies, it bears much fruit. Those who love their life lose it, and those who hate their life in this world will keep it for eternal life. Whoever serves me must follow me, and where I am, there will my servant be also. Whoever serves me, the Father will honour.[6]

As with all his parables, Jesus is revealing a meaning embedded within nature herself, which expresses a single truth on many parallel levels. Central to all these meanings and levels, and clearly central in the context of this parable in John, is a teaching about the meaning and purpose of Jesus' own imminent death, and a promise of his resurrection. He himself, who has earlier said "I am the bread of life" now concentrates all he is and all he offers into a single grain and says "I am willing to be cast away and fallen for you, you will seem to lose me, I will be buried and covered over but because I do this for you, because you are in me and I in you, I will not remain a single grain and neither will you. But by my dying you and I, no longer single grains, will bear much fruit."

If the self-sacrifice of the cross is foreshadowed and expressed in the falling of the single grain to the earth, then the rich promise and sheer transformation of the resurrection is expressed in the way that single grain, seemingly so isolated and covered in its husk, is raised in all the complexity and beauty of the living plant. This single saying of Jesus is surely itself the grain and seed that flowers in Paul's great teaching about the Resurrection in 1 Corinthians—that Christ is the first fruits of those who sleep, and that the risen body is so much more than what was sown in death:

So it is with the resurrection of the dead. What is sown is perishable, what is raised is imperishable. It is sown in dishonour, it is raised in glory. It is sown in weakness, it is raised in power. It is sown a physical body, it is raised a spiritual body.[7]

The Sower, a lithograph by Jean-François Millet

Again it is not a coincidence that Jesus happens to find in the sowing of a seed and in the raising of new growth such a perfect analogy for his death and resurrection. For, as the *Logos*, he so ordered the cosmos that there should be everywhere, not only in the sowing of seed and the new growth of a plant, but in the way day follows night, and spring follows winter, there should be always and everywhere the pattern of his redemptive love, which is the pattern of death and resurrection. As the letter to the Colossians affirmed:

> He is the image of the invisible God, the firstborn of all creation; for in him all things in heaven and on earth were created, things visible and invisible, whether thrones or dominions or rulers or powers—all things have been created through him and for him. He himself is before all things, and in him all things hold together.[8]

We had always seen that pattern, everywhere in every faith and culture, and responded to it imaginatively and now the Word comes into our midst as one of us and shows us what it really means.

But there is more. Precisely because this image or parable of the seed in the ground shows the meaning of Christ's death and resurrection, so it also teaches us about ourselves and our own way of living, that is to say it kindles our moral imagination. For Christ is not only teaching the disciples how he will die, he is teaching them how they should live! Immediately after giving them the image of the grain in verse 24 he goes on in verse 25 to say

> Those who love their life lose it, those who hate their life in this world will keep it for eternal life. Whoever serves me must follow me, and where I am, there will my servant be also.[9]

And so he discloses the great truth we have always known, but always shied away from: that love must never cling, dominate, or possess even the self, let alone others, but rather constantly let go in order to receive back all that has been relinquished. But what we receive back is transformed: it is no longer a possession but a gift.

Can poetry, and the arts more widely, help us unfold a little more of what is happening in this parable? Now here I am going to be personal and draw from some of my own poetry.

In the autumn of 2014 I started a sequence of sonnets on the sayings of Jesus called *Parable and Paradox*. I began that sequence whilst I was artist-in-residence at Duke Divinity School and the then Dean of that School, the great New Testament scholar, Richard Hays, lent me his study for the time I was there. The first poem I wrote (although not the first in the published sequence) was composed in his study reflecting on this very verse:

The Sower (The Parables of Our Lord and Saviour Jesus Christ), a wood engraving by John Everett Millais

A Grain of Wheat

*John 12:24: Unless a grain of wheat falls into the earth and dies,
it remains just a single grain; but if it dies, it bears much fruit.*

Oh let me fall as grain to the good earth
And die away from all dry separation,
Die to my sole self, and find new birth
Within that very death, a dark fruition
Deep in this crowded underground, to learn
The earthy otherness of every other,
To know that nothing is achieved alone
But only where these other fallen gather.

If I bear fruit and break through to bright air,
Then fall upon me with your freeing flail
To shuck this husk and leave me sheer and clear
As heaven-handled Hopkins, that my fall
May be more fruitful and my autumn still
A golden evening where your barns are full.[10]

As a poet, I did not feel I had to choose between the levels at which this image of the seed is working. And yet responding to the parable with poetry aroused my moral imagination, my capacity to re-imagine my sense of self in a way that would allow me to let go and so to receive. So in the first instance, Christ's teaching made me imagine myself as the grain:

Oh let me fall as grain to the good earth
And die away from all dry separation,
Die to my sole self,

But this re-imagination of self was made possible for me by the fact that Christ has also imagined himself as the grain and, indeed, in the most profound sense become that grain. I did not have to choose as to whether my poem was about all the particular "dyings away" from selfishness and separation that constitute new life in the kingdom or whether it was about my own mortality. It was always, necessarily, about both. My final image of a fall made fruitful, of the golden evening and the full barn, was about *both* the possibility of being fruitful in this life *and* about our resurrection.

But in the case of this poem rather than offer you my own interpretation, (for as Socrates observed poets are usually the last people who know what is going on in their own poems), I would like to let Richard Hays himself open up this poem for you and here I need to tell you a remarkable story.

At about the same time that Richard was taking a sabbatical break and lending his room to me, he was diagnosed with pancreatic cancer. Quite understandably he and his family and friends saw little hope of his living much longer and he began to set his house and his life in order and ready himself for the end. In fact, by great medical skill, by a surrounding of prayer, and by a turn of events which I think reasonable to call miraculous, he pulled through and was eventually able to return to that study and his life at Duke. In due course he did retire and gave a remarkable valedictory address. Although I had dedicated *Parable and Paradox* to him, and he had kindly accepted the dedication, he did not know at the time he composed his address that this particular poem was the first I had written in his room and had set the whole sequence in train. But he chose to call his address "A Dark Fruition,"[11] borrowing a phrase from my poem, and in that address he offered a remarkable reading both of this teaching of Jesus and of my effort to re-imagine it in the poem.

Hays begins with a response to the parable itself:

> This parable of Jesus resonates with chords that echo throughout the [New Testament]. Jesus' impending death is to be not futile but fruitful. Jesus himself is the Word sown into the good dark earth. *He* is the single grain that falls into the earth and dies, and so yields a rich harvest. *His* faithfulness—the faithfulness of Jesus Christ—unto death on a cross will become life-giving for others. Everything depends on *his* self-giving, not on our efforts or on our intelligence, not even on our faith.
>
> But right along with that proclamation, he calls his hearers to follow after him; he challenges them to surrender their own lives, not to clutch them possessively. And he promises that those who follow will be *with* him, not only in death but also the life of the resurrection; they will be part of the rich harvest. That is the challenge, and the promise, that Dietrich Bonhoeffer echoed in *The Cost of Discipleship*, a book that influenced me powerfully when Judy and I first read it together, almost fifty years ago. Bonhoeffer wrote, "When Christ calls a man, he bids him come and die."

Then he turns to my poem:

As I have lived a little deeper into my autumn years, I have made Malcolm's sonnet my own prayer, my own response to Jesus' promise and summons... now when I hear Jesus speak of the grain that must fall into the earth and die, I understand him to mean something that is both more literal and more radically transformative. It is not merely a matter of exchanging an inadequate self-understanding for a better one. It is a matter of letting go of life itself, of entering the mystery of death and resurrection. My own brush with literal death has deepened my conviction that our hope lies in our union with Christ and in the ultimate promise of resurrection of the body. That is what I mean by suggesting that Jesus' saying is more literal—for us, just as it was for him. He really was about to die. We too will die. And, as Jesus was raised from the dead, so too will we be raised with him.

But Jesus' saying about the grain is also more radically *transformative* than I understood at age nineteen. For those who follow Jesus, his pattern of death followed by fruit-bearing becomes a *typos,* a pattern that remolds *everything* in the life we still live in this mortal flesh. Dying in order to bear fruit is not something that happens once at a moment of conversion. It happens over the span of a life....

Malcom Guite's sonnet gently exhumes an insight that could all too easily lie buried in the Greek text of John 12. Jesus says, "Unless a grain of wheat falls into the earth and dies, it remains just a single grain." That's the New Revised Standard Version; most modern English translations make a similar, semantically justifiable, translation decision. But the Greek text carries an additional connotation. Here's what it says: "Unless a grain of wheat falls into the earth and dies, *autos monos menei":* literally, "it remains *alone."* The King James Version rendered the phrase as "it abideth alone." That's a good translation; it not only catches the force of *monos* as "alone, solitary," but also highlights the Greek text's verbal link to Jesus' later contrasting invitation, in his farewell address to his disciples, the invitation to *abide* in him. Same verb in the Greek.

The first eight lines of Guite's sonnet highlight the way in which the death of the grain of wheat is a movement *away from* loneliness and *into* community. The poet prays, "Oh let me .die *away from all dry separation, /* Die *to my sole self."* Indeed the expression "sole self" deftly echoes John's Greek: *autos monos.*

And the praying voice of the sonnet envisions that the place of dark fruition is not a solitary dark tomb; instead, "deep in this *crowded* underground," alongside many other grains, the poet will learn "*the earthy otherness of every other.*" It is precisely through learning that "earthy otherness," then, that he comes "To know that nothing is achieved alone / But only where these other fallen gather."

What better description could there be of the church? It is a place where "these other fallen gather," and where, like it or not, we rub up against the earthy otherness of every other. Whatever we achieve there, we will not achieve it alone, but only alongside other earthy creatures who gather to follow a Lord who humbled himself all the way to death on a cross.

Hays concludes:

In our life together as *community,* even in the midst of our groaning, we have tasted the first fruits of the Spirit. That is why, even in a time of dark fruition, we wait in hope.

It was a remarkable experience for me to read Richard Hays' lecture, not only because he expounded my poem so well, but because his lecture made me realise that the imagination at work in me when I wrote the poem was not simply my own. Christ had given me in this parable an image to work with, an image that is older and wiser than I am. He had, of course, given Richard Hays that same image. But more than that: the *Logos,* himself, who has become Jesus, has shaped Richard's mind and mine, and of course yours too, so that we might receive Christ's images fruitfully. Some years ago I was on a panel with the Irish poet Micheal O'Siadhail, when he was asked whether he thought his poetry ever sowed the seed of the Gospel. "Oh, goodness no," he said,

I'd never presume that. But if you are referring with that phrase to the Parable of the Sower, I take it that the one who sows the seed is the Word himself, and the seed also is the Word, but what interests me is how much attention that parable pays to the condition of the soil. The soil in my own garden needs to be taken up and shaken in a riddle to remove loose stones, to let in the air, so that it becomes good ground for receiving seed. My poems may not sow seeds, but at their best I hope they jostle the soil of the imagination so that it is ready to receive that seed which is the Word, sown by the Word.[12]

What Richard Hays' Lecture showed me was that my poem had somehow, by God's grace, jostled the soil of his imagination just as his close reading of the scripture had jostled the soil of mine.

The Good Samaritan Tending the Traveller's Wounds with Oil and Wine or *The Priest and the Levite Passing,*
an engraving by Heinrich Aldegrever

Appealing to the Moral Imagination

We have touched on the way this parable, although so centrally about Christ himself, nevertheless rouses and appeals to the moral imagination, and I would like to spend the rest of this chapter developing that thought. But first, we must ask, what is the moral imagination? I would say that it is particularly that exercise of imagination which enables you to stand in another person's shoes, to go out from your life and place and into theirs, to imagine and even re-imagine the world from their perspective. It is this act of imagination that is at the core of Jesus' central moral teaching, summed up in the Golden Rule: "Do to others as you would have them do to you."[13] This core teaching is then developed in several ways in Jesus' more elaborate parables, most explicitly perhaps in the parable of the Good Samaritan. And before we turn to a powerful poetic handling of that parable, I want to remark on Jesus' own authority to invoke our moral imaginations in this way. Just as the parable of the grain of wheat, which seemed to be primarily about Jesus himself, about his death and resurrection, turned out to be morally transformative for us, so too the parables of the kingdom and the other parables which seem to be about our "moral" response to one another, turn out also to be about Jesus, because he *is* the Kingdom he proclaims! He already is, and always enacts whatever he asks of us. If the awakened moral imagination calls and enables us to change place and perspective, if Jesus in speaking these parables calls us to die to ourselves and live to others, then he does so with authority because that is what he himself has done, not just imaginatively but actually in his incarnation, death, and resurrection. He leaves heaven, empties himself for love of us, and chooses to look at the world through our eyes and from our perspective.

Piers Plowman and the Parable of the Good Samaritan

And now let us turn to the Parable of the Good Samaritan. I would like to approach this familiar parable through a poem which may be less familiar: William Langland's great fourteenth-century allegorical poem in alliterative verse, *Piers Plowman*. It is written in Middle English, but for clarity I am going to quote Henry Wells' rendition into modern English, which happily keeps most of the alliteration and meter. The poem is a series of dream-visions narrated by a dreamer who is, in some sense, a proxy for the reader, an "everyman" with whom we can identify. In the course of his pilgrimage through life, the dreamer meets up with a character called "Hope" (*Spes* in the poem), and another one called "Faith," though he knows that there must be a third friend to go along with Hope and Faith whom he has not yet found. Suddenly they find themselves witnessing the story of the Good Samaritan:

> As we went on the way talking together
> We saw a Samaritan sitting in his saddle,
> Riding rapidly on the road that we had taken,
> Coming from a country that men call Jericho,
> And hastening on his way to a joust in Jerusalem.
> He overtook the herald and Hope together,
> Where a man was wounded and waylaid by robbers.
> He could neither stand not stir nor signal for assistance,
> Nor in any way save himself, and seemed half perished,
> Naked as a needle and no help about him.[14]

You will see that, already, with his talk of jousting, Langland has given the story a setting that was contemporary to him, in the chivalric culture of the High Middle Ages, when you really could meet knights in armour on their way to a joust. But then the poetic imagination, the allegorical frame and a deep

The Ploughman, a wood engraving by Edward Calvert

theological insight allow him to open out Jesus' story in a new way. For instead of the Priest and the Levite being the ones who cross over to the other side of the road, and seem unable by themselves to help the man, in Langland's telling it is Faith and Hope who, left to themselves, fail the test:

> Faith had first sight of him but veered around him,
> And would not come near him by nine furrows.
> Hope came hastening after. He had already boasted
> How he had helped many men with Moses' covenant.
> But when he saw that sight he stepped sidewise
> As much in dread, by this day, as a duck of a falcon![15]

And then Langland brings the Samaritan centre-stage. He enters this medieval setting as a kind of chivalrous knight errant, and we begin to feel there is more to this Samaritan than meets the eye:

> But as soon as the Samaritan saw the sick man
> He alighted from his horse and led him by the bridle
> And went to that wanderer, found his wounds open,
> And perceived by his pulse that he was at the point of dying;
> That unless a saviour came speedily he should not rise live.
> He unbuckled his two bottles and poured both together,
> He washed his wounds with wine and oil,

Anointed him and bound his head and carried him carefully
And held him upon his horse till they arrived at *Lex Christi*,
An inn six or seven miles this side the New Market.
He harboured him in the hostelry and called the host to him

The Good Samaritan (Barmherziger Samariter), a woodcut by Ernst Barlach

And said: "If he spends further, I shall make good hereafter
For I may not stay," he said; and bestrode his charger,
And so rode rapidly on the highroad to Jerusalem.[16]

Since Faith and Hope have fled, the dreamer comes up to the Samaritan and asks to be his ostler and look after his horse. In a lovely touch and with a hint of what is to come, the Samaritan tells him that the horse is "*Caro* my courser which mankind supplied me" (*Caro* of course means flesh, as in *verbum caro factum est*).[17] The two then, rather astonishingly, have a long discussion of the Trinity, and the Samaritan advises the dreamer that he should never close his heart to anyone, but should look for the image of the Trinity in them, it is the light and life in everyone, for:

The Holy Ghost has in keeping what the heartless ravish,
The life and the love which is the light of a man's body.
For every kind of good man may be compared in simile
To a torch or a taper to reference the Trinity[18]

The Sleeper, who it turns out is one of the homeless poor, awakes:

In woollen clothes and wet-shod I
Walked forth afterwards,
As a reckless wretch who reckons not suffering.
I went forth like a vagrant for all my lifetime,[19]

But happily he dreams again and this time he finds himself a witness to the events of Palm Sunday and sees at last who the Samaritan really is:

One similar to the Samaritan and sometimes to Piers the Plowman
Came barefoot on an ass's back, bootless yet pricking.
He had no spurs nor spear, but was sprightly in bearing.
Like a squire speeding to the ceremony of knighthood
To get his gilt spurs and cut goloshes.
Then Faith cried from his window, "*A, fili David!*"
As an herald in arms when adventurers come to jousting.
Old Jews in Jerusalem joyously chorused:
Benedictus qui venit in nomine Domini.

Then I asked Faith aside what affair was stirring,
And who should joust in Jerusalem. "Jesus," he answered,[20]

And so the poem goes on to describe the Passion, as a joust and victory against "the foul fiend, falsehood and death."[21]

There is a great deal to be said about the skill and depth with which the story is being handled here, and to do so fully would require even longer extracts from the poem and a major excursus into medieval dream poetry, but for our purpose here I just want to make three brief observations.

The first is that Langland feels a complete freedom to re-imagine Jesus' own imagined story freshly in his own context, to frame it amidst stories of knights and jousting, and to imagine the inn as "not far from New Market." Newmarket is about seventeen miles from where I live! It is also a nice touch that, having

Return of the Prodigal Son, an etching by Rembrandt Harmenszoon van Rijn

given the hostelry such a down to earth location, Langland goes on to give it an allegorical name—the Inn is called *Lex Christi*—the Law of Christ, that is to say the new commandment of Love. So here we see how one act of creative imagination kindles and invites another, but the imaginative response, far from making the story less real, actually brings it home to us. My second observation is that although the allegory deepens and adds many layers, it does not in any way overwrite the central moral purpose of the story as a call to compassion. Finally, there is a beautiful sequence in the way the story is told, in which, by means of a series of clues, and finally a moment of epiphany or recognition, we are shown that the story of the Good Samaritan, just like the parable of the Grain of Wheat, is another telling of the Incarnation and saving Passion of Jesus.

All the parables of Jesus are of course a hugely generative gift to other artists and writers as well as to poets, and this is precisely because the parables work with image, story, and emblem: the very stuff of the creative arts. There is always a parallel in a parable, always some sense in which the outward and visible story translates the inward and spiritual into new and imaginatively and generous terms. That story is itself translatable, translatable from story into image, translatable across time and culture. Since the time of the Gospels, countless artists have availed themselves of the principle of parable, some have done so by a direct concentration of the actual story Jesus tells, just as Langland did with the parable of the Good Samaritan, so in another art form Rembrandt does in *Return of the Prodigal Son*.

As in his famous oil painting with the same title and subject in the Hermitage, this engraving has Rembrandt offering us a discreet and delicate yet fully incarnational imaginative response to Jesus' parable. He chooses to portray in both this engraving and in the painting the moment of embrace and welcome to the son, with the son's face buried and pressed into the bosom of his father, overshadowed by his welcoming and cloak, half-concealed from the others in the picture, as though that tender moment of return is too intimate to be portrayed. In the etching he is shoeless and ragged, and in the painting the soles of the prodigal's shoes are utterly worn, one of the soles shredded, his foot marked and hurt by the stumbles of his return journey. In these pieces we feel we are looking not simply at a portrait of the soles of this suffering man, but of the soul itself.

For other artists and writers the invitation of Jesus' parables is not so much to concentrate on the stories Jesus told as to follow his example and to go out and make new stories which are also capable of embodying inward truth, as Coleridge put it,

...to transfer from our inward nature a human interest and a semblance of truth sufficient to procure for these shadows of imagination that willing suspension of disbelief for the moment, which constitutes poetic faith.[22]

George MacDonald, J.R.R. Tolkien, and C.S. Lewis are writers of this type. They tell wonderful stories which are well worth reading in their own right, and are consistent and beautiful in their own imagined world. And yet, although they are not complete or formal allegories, they are infinitely suggestive and they are full of what Lewis called "incipient allegories." Their episodes and images mediate Gospel truths to us in fresh and surprising ways because, through the medium of story, their authors have lifted the veil, removed the film of familiarity, and allowed an ancient truth to strike us in a fresh and immediate way. We certainly need new imaginative artists to take up afresh that task of unveiling and renewal through daring acts of re-imagination.

Parable of the Good Shepherd (after Pieter Bruegel the Elder), an engraving by Philips Galle

The Call to Imagine: a Personal Response

In the last part of this chapter I want to return to my own personal experience in responding with poetry to the parables and paradoxes of Jesus.

The more I worked on the *Parable and Paradox* sequence the more I realised how constantly Jesus' teaching appeals to the imagination, even when it does not seem, explicitly, to be doing so. For example, in the verse just before the Golden Rule which we quoted earlier from Luke, Jesus gives a teaching which seems straightforward and without analogy, and yet it is so shocking and seemingly contrary to our nature that it calls on us completely to re-imagine ourselves:

> Give to everyone who begs from you; and if anyone takes away
> your goods, do not ask for them again.[23]

Here is the response which that saying evoked in me:

As If
The Giver of all gifts asks *me* to give!
The Fountain from which every good thing flows,
The Life who spends himself that all might live,
The Root whence every bud and blossom grows,
Calls me, as if I knew no limitation,
As if I focused all his hidden force,
To be creative with his new creation,
To find my flow in him, my living source,
To live as if I had no fear of losing,
To spend as if I had no need to earn,
To turn my cheek as if it felt no bruising,
To lend as if I needed no return,
As if my debts and sins were all forgiven,
As if I too could body forth his heaven.[24]

As I wrote this poem, with its strong rhythms, its list of verbs in the infinitive—*to find, to live, to spend, to turn, to lend*—and with its repeated litany of the phrase *as if*, I realised that this poem was in some sense being haunted by another more famous poem to which it was replying. By the time I had written the last line I knew what that poem was: it was Rudyard Kipling's "*If.*"[25] Now, "*If*" is a great poem and indeed was recently voted Britain's favourite poem (perhaps this is not surprising as we are a nation of Pelagians), but I realised I had always felt that, for all its rhetorical vigour, there is something dark and shadowed about Kipling's long list of conditions. All those "ifs" summed up in the final one:

If you can fill the unforgiving minute
With sixty seconds' worth of distance run,[26]

And *if* you can do and achieve in your own strength all these nearly impossible things, what then? What is your reward?

Yours is the Earth and everything that's in it,
And—which is more—you'll be a Man, my son![27]

And I suddenly saw that, powerful as it is, Kipling's poem is the exact opposite of the Gospel! It is a poem of *conditional* love, in some ways a horrific poem in which a father sets impossible conditions for his son, and a son desperately completes all kinds of tasks to try and earn his father's love, so as to be awarded at last the right to be called "my son." And even those tasks are none of them labouring for the Kingdom, but merely honing one's good business and colonial skills in order to seize on this world's goods: "the Earth and everything that's in it." Whereas, the Gospel is the Good News that our Father already loves us as his children *unconditionally,* whatever we do or don't achieve. He does not say I will only love you *if* you do these things, he treats us already *as if* we had done and achieved the things we accuse ourselves for failing in. We are beloved *already* and he delights in us. Insofar as his love inspires us to good deeds or acts in thankfulness, their primary aim is not to gain the Earth and everything that's in it but rather to seek the Kingdom of God and his righteousness:

> ...indeed your heavenly Father knows that you need all these things. But strive first for the kingdom of God and his righteousness, and all these things will be given to you as well.[28]

"All these things" are not a reward for labour but are the sheer gift of God's good creation which we delight in with him, not as cold owners, but as fellow makers and shapers.

I realised as I wrote this poem that Jesus was inviting me to use, playfully, those phrases the imagination loves to use: *as if, what if, imagine that . . .* Jesus asks me to live *as if* all my playful "as ifs" were already true. And, of course, when I got to the penultimate line of my sonnet, I realised one of them already was:

As if my debit and sins were all forgiven.

But they are!

When I first titled this poem *As If* I had imagined that phrase might be read with a tone of mocking skepticism, "*as* if," but by the end of the poem the same phrase could be uttered in tones of glad surprise. I realised that Jesus might invite me so to imagine the Kingdom, that somehow, between the two of us, it might start coming true.

This insight, fairly early in the poetic sequence, led me to embrace the word *imagine*, and in allusion to John Lennon's famous song, to call one of my poems "Imagine." That poem was also responding to a verse in this same chapter of Luke:

Imagine
Luke 6:37: Do not judge, and you will not be judged; do not condemn, and you will not be condemned. Forgive, and you will be forgiven.

Do not judge, and you will not be judged.
Imagine if we took these words to heart,
Unselved ourselves and took another's part,
Silenced the accuser, dropped the grudge ...
Do not condemn, you will not be condemned.
Imagine if we lived our lives from this
And met each other's outcasts face to face,
Imagine if the blood-dimmed tide was stemmed.
Forgive and you yourselves will be forgiven.
What if we walked together on this path,
What if the whole world laid aside its wrath,
And things were done on earth as though in heaven,
As though the heart's dark knots were all undone,
As though this dreamer weren't the only one?[29]

With sublime indifference to the ways of the world, happily ignoring all the usual cycles of self-justifying judgmentalism and self-righteous finger-pointing, setting aside, as though they had never happened, the myriad ways in which we all keep score, Jesus simply initiates for us a whole new way of being with each other. He asks us to live and look at the world as though this new approach were the most natural thing in the world, which it actually is, but we have forgotten our true nature. And because we have forgotten our true nature, everything has to be imagined and re-imagined.

In this poem the question the imagination loves to ask is *what if?* and the phrase it loves to use is *as though*:

What if we walked together on this path,
What if the whole world laid aside its wrath,
And things were done on earth *as though* in heaven,

In Yeats' poem "The Second Coming" he saw clear-sightedly what our fallen
and forgetful natures were doing to the world:

Things fall apart; the centre cannot hold;
Mere anarchy is loosed upon the world,
The blood-dimmed tide is loosed,[30]

Arma Christi, a linocut by Ned Bustard

But Yeats' "The Second Coming" is not the one to which Christians are looking forward, not the great hope of the Kingdom, and so I felt moved to reply to Yeats:

Imagine if the blood-dimmed tide *was stemmed.*

For I believe it has been stemmed, was stemmed when, in the words of the poet John Heath-Stubbs:

A stake was stemmed in the rubbish[31]

For the Son of God was raised aloft on the cross, that stake stemmed in the rubbish, and took into himself all the evil ever loosed upon the world and replied to it with love.

And, as I mentioned, I also felt moved in this poem to reply to John Lennon. Now I love "Imagine" simply as a song and I applaud the longing that motivated Lennon to write it: the longing that there really should be "no need for greed or hunger," and, in the unfortunately non-inclusive language of the day, the longing that there should be "a brotherhood of man." But as with Kipling's *"If,"* I felt there was a contradiction at the heart of Lennon's song and, indeed, even in its opening words: "Imagine there's no heaven." In fact, what Lennon is asking us to do in that song is precisely to imagine a kind of heaven, to exercise our moral imaginations, to conjure up the vision of a way of living, which we cannot actually see in action, but which we know should exist. I regret that, for entirely understandable reasons to do with the kind of church life he encountered as a child, Lennon thought that Christianity was part of the problem and not part of the solution. But, in fact, you cannot "imagine there's no heaven," for to imagine at all is to open yourself up to the possibilities of heaven. Indeed what we are shown in the Gospels is the wonderful event in which the heart of heaven himself comes to earth and enables and inspires us to do that imagining. He does it most vividly, most powerfully and most radically in the Beatitudes, in which he asks us to imagine a way of living that turns the whole world upside down, or if we understand more deeply, right way up at last. But to open up the Beatitudes we must move from the moral to the prophetic imagination, and that is the purpose of the next chapter.

NOTES

1   Psalm 1:3

2   Samuel Taylor Coleridge, "Frost at Midnight," in *The Complete Poetical Works of Samuel Taylor Coleridge*, Vol. I: Poems, ed. Ernest Hartley Coleridge (Oxford: Clarendon Press, 1912), pp. 240–242, lines 59–64.

3   Samuel Taylor Coleridge, *Biographia Literaria*, ed. James Engell and W. Jackson Bate (Princeton, NJ: Princeton University Press), vol. I, p. 304.

4   Ibid.

5   Coleridge, "Frost at Midnight," pp. 240–242, lines 59–60.

6   John 12:23–26.

7   1 Corinthians 15:42–45.

8   Colossians 1:15–17.

9   John 12:25–26 (part).

10 Malcolm Guite, "A Grain of Wheat," in *Parable and Paradox: Sonnets on the Sayings of Jesus and Other Poems* (London, UK: Canterbury Press, 2016), p. 63.

11 On 25th September 2018, Duke Divinity School hosted a retirement lecture given by Richard Hays, George Washington Ivey Professor Emeritus of New Testament and former dean of the Divinity School. This is a link to a recording of that lecture: https://divinity.duke.edu/news/watch-richard-hayss-retirement-lecture. Also included in *Reading with the Grain of Scripture*, by Richard B. Hays (Grand Rapids, MI: William B. Eerdman's Publishing Co., 2020).

12 Here I am paraphrasing his words from memory.

13 Luke 6:31.

14 William Langland, *The Vision of Piers Plowman*, trans. Henry W. Wells (New York: Greenwood Press, 1968), lines 48–57.

15 Langland, *Piers Plowman*, lines 58–63.

16 Langland, lines 64–80.

17 The Latin translates as "and the word was made flesh."

18 Langland, lines 281–284.

19 Langland, *Piers Plowman*, Passus XVIII, lines 1–3.

20 Langland, lines 10–20.

21 Langland, line 29.

22 Coleridge, *Biographia Literaria*, vol. II, p. 6.

23 Luke 6:30.

24 Guite, "As If," in *Parable and Paradox*, p. 31.

25 Rudyard Kipling, "If"—written circa 1895, first published in *Rewards and Fairies* (1910).

26 Kipling, "If," lines 28–29.

27 Kipling, lines 30–end.

28 Matthew 6:32–33.

29 Guite, "Imagine," in *Parable and Paradox*, p. 46.

30 W.B. Yeats, "The Second Coming"—written in 1919, first printed in *The Dial* in November 1920 then in Yeats' 1921 book *Michael Robartes and the Dancer*, lines 3–6.

31 John Heath-Stubbs, "Golgotha," in *Selected Poems*, (Manchester, UK: Carcanet Classics, 1990), p. 55, line 3.

CHRIST
and the
PROPHETIC
IMAGINATION

THE IMAGINATION UNVEILS hidden reality, clarifies vision, and gives substance to hope. In this chapter on Christ and the prophetic imagination I want to speak of how that visionary hope itself enables the two other aspects of prophetic utterance: speaking truth to power, and foretelling or foreshadowing what is to come. But before we engage in any analysis of the prophetic voice in its many scriptural and theological modes, I'd like to explore what it means to speak of imagining the Kingdom, to have what Walter Brueggemann[1] called *The Prophetic Imagination.*

Christ is constantly inviting us to imagine, and so to encounter, the Kingdom of God. He proclaims that the Kingdom of God is at hand, and teaches us to pray that it should come. In every word, in every gesture he shows us what the Kingdom is, since he himself bodies it forth. To imagine the Kingdom is always a prophetic act, always a critique of this world, always a call to hope and action. Before we turn to the vision of the Kingdom and its values that Jesus shares in the Sermon on the Mount and specifically in the Beatitudes, I'd like to share with you a short poem responding to those Beatitudes, in which R.S. Thomas, a great twentieth-century poet, imagines the Kingdom. It is a poem in which many of the themes we will later develop are memorably embodied:

The Vision of God, an engraving from *Illustrations of the Book of Job* by William Blake

The Kingdom
It's a long way off but inside it
There are quite different things going on:
Festivals at which the poor man
Is king and the consumptive is
Healed; mirrors in which the blind look
At themselves and love looks at them
Back; and industry is for mending
The bent bones and the minds fractured
By life. It's a long way off, but to get
There takes no time and admission
Is free, if you purge yourself
Of desire, and present yourself with
Your need only and the simple offering
Of your faith, green as a leaf.[2]

There is so much going on in this sonnet, so much that Thomas has absorbed from Christ's teaching and his parables of the Kingdom. Here is a poem which reflects back for us in vivid imagery the strange reversals of Christ's Kingdom: the last being made first, the poor blessed, the eyes of the blind opened—and not opened randomly—but opened so that they may look on love, who looks on them. It's a poem that sees into the core of Christ's mission, and that core is redemption: not the *ending* but rather the *mending* all that is bent and fractured in our fall. It's a poem that is realistic about the despairing sense we have of distance and difference when we contemplate the Kingdom. We hear the Sermon on the Mount, and we see how absolutely and radically different it is from the way we do things now: the way we have imagined things so far. Because it is so different, we cannot help but feel that it is distant, that our world seems so bent awry, so obviously travelling in the wrong direction, that we can never get there. Thomas seems to concede this in the very opening words of his poem "It's a long way off" but at the *volta* or turning point in his sonnet he returns to that phrase and this time offers us hope:

> It's a long way off, but to get
> There takes no time and admission
> Is free,[3]

And so, as with all the paradoxes of Jesus, we are offered a possible impossibility. And what is in the offer?

> inside it
> There are quite different things going on[4]

How is that difference expressed? Thomas takes three familiar things from our secular lives and offers them up to be transformed in and through the imagination of the Kingdom—festivals, mirrors, and industry:

> *Festivals* at which the poor man
> Is king and the consumptive is
> Healed; *mirrors* in which the blind look
> At themselves and love looks at them
> Back; and *industry* is for mending
> The bent bones and the minds fractured
> By life.[5]

Festivals

Our own festivals are many and various, but certainly at our musical, cultural, and sporting festivals those who are enthroned and exalted on the stage and in the arena are in some sense kings already, they are the accoladed, the stars and the heroes. Accustomed to the world's praises, they are lifted up at each festival to receive a little more manna; they are always the known performing to the unknown, the rich enriched a little further by the comparatively poor. Not so in the festivals of the Kingdom:

> Festivals at which the poor man
> Is king and the consumptive is
> Healed;[6]

At the festivals of the Kingdom, Christ the King himself takes the form of a servant that he might share the cross of the poor and offer his crown to them in return. The festivals of the church year are meant to be anticipations of the festivals of the Kingdom, though we might miss that amidst the church's pomp and ceremony. Thomas may have been thinking of an old festival we no longer keep: All Fools' Day, in which masters served their servants for a day and in the cathedrals the youngest and most foolish of the choirboys became "the boy bishop."

Urban Nativity for John, a charcoal drawing by Wayne Forte

But in the Kingdom, this is no mere playful reversal for a day, not one of those ritual reversals, which end up emphasising and confirming the status quo, but rather its reversal is the setting for true healing and permanent transformation:

> … the consumptive is
> Healed;[7]

Thomas's choice of the consumptive as the instance of Kingdom healing is interesting here; a lesser poet would have chosen almost automatically one of the biblical examples and perhaps even the specific examples cited by Jesus when he sends his message to encourage the imprisoned John the Baptist with the signs of the Kingdom.

> When John heard in prison what the Messiah was doing, he sent word by his disciples and said to him, "Are you the one who is to come, or are we to wait for another?" Jesus answered them, "Go and tell John what you hear and see: the blind receive their sight, the lame walk, the lepers are cleansed, the deaf hear, the dead are raised, and the poor have good news brought to them.[8]

Of course, that passage, with its mention of the poor and the blind, is partly echoed by Thomas in this poem, as is the moment in the synagogue when Jesus reads from Prophet Isaiah and declares the Isaiah's prophetic vision of the Messiah inaugurating the Kingdom is fulfilled in his coming:

> "The Spirit of the Lord is upon me, because he has anointed me to bring good news to the poor. He has sent me to proclaim release to the captives and recovery of sight to the blind, to let the oppressed go free, to proclaim the year of the Lord's favor." And he rolled up the scroll, gave it back to the attendant, and sat down. The eyes of all in the synagogue were fixed on him. Then he began to say to them, "Today this scripture has been fulfilled in your hearing."[9]

But had Thomas only echoed these passages, there might have been a danger that the focus of this twentieth-century poem would have receded back to a kind of Sunday School never-never land of "scripture." But by saying "the consumptive is / healed," Thomas says something different. At one level, of course, we think of the consumptive specifically as the person with tuberculosis, a scourge that was still just present in Britain when Thomas was writing and which, perhaps, had particular resonance for him as a poet when one thinks of the poets who were not healed of it, particularly George Herbert and John Keats.

But I think the word "consumptive" suggests more than that, especially as it is followed so soon in the poem by the word "industry." For although the consumptive is so called because he is in some sense consumed and overwhelmed by his illness and suffocated by what his own body produces, there is another sense in which our whole contemporary culture suffers from, and is suffocated by consumption, or rather over-consumption. It is against the consumerism of the rich that "the quite different things going on" in "the Kingdom" are set. So when we are told that in the festivals of the Kingdom the consumptive is healed, we and our whole way of living are challenged and included in that healing.

Mirrors

And then Thomas offers us the image of "mirrors," and again the secular image is challenged, redeemed, and transfigured in "The Kingdom." Our secular mirrors are associated with vanity both in the modern trivial sense of obsessive care for and interest in our personal appearance, but also in the deeper biblical sense of *vanitas* or nothingness:

> Vanity of vanities, saith the Preacher, vanity of vanities; all is vanity. What profit hath a man of all his labour which he taketh under the sun?[10]

But in "The Kingdom" the mirrors are not for the sighted to see nothing but themselves, but for the blind to see themselves at last, as God sees them. But, following Herbert, Thomas eschews the word "God" and uses the word "Love":

> ... mirrors in which the blind look
> At themselves and love looks at them
> Back;[11]

Thomas is here perhaps drawing on the Christian mystical tradition in works like "The Mirror of Perfection," in which Christ is seen as the mirror that holds God's image and also allows us to see ourselves, at last, as we should be: found and perfected in him. But he does more than that. In this world our mirrors are essentially empty "mere mirrors" and not windows: we look into them, but, for all the illusion of a face, nothing and no one actually looks back. The word "mirror" is a borrowing from French, via Anglo-Norman, and the more usual English word was "glass." Thomas is almost certainly thinking of the great passage in 1 Corinthians as it was translated in the King James Version:

> For now we see through a glass, darkly; but then face to face: now
> I know in part; but then shall I know even as also I am known.[12]

In Thomas's prophetic imagination of the Kingdom, the dark glass brightens at last and we find ourselves face-to-face with the face of Love.

Industry

Just as his choice of the word "consumptive" brought us out of "Bibleland" and into our more familiar world, so the word "industry" centres us in the modern industrial world. Of course, the word 'industry' itself simply denotes productive labour, but it also carries for us the connotation of the vast mechanised processes which fuel our consumption. And here, "The Kingdom" offers us a double reversal, a double renewal. Thomas ends line seven "and industry is for mending": that in itself is a reversal. We all know that in fact modern consumerism is predicated on built-in obsolescence and on not mending things but rather on trashing them and buying new ones. Things that are made at home, or by hand, can be mended at home and by hand, but more and more, even more so now than in Thomas's day, the "captains of industry" have designed things so they are un-mendable and must be replace with more consumption.[13]

Perhaps we are prepared for this reversal in the purpose of industry by the image of mirrors that precedes it, for in mirrors all things are reversed. But there is more, for in the Kingdom, industry is not simply for mending *things* but for mending *people*: for mending "the bent bones and the minds fractured by life." Again there is redemption at work. For the actual effect of the Industrial Revolution on the labouring poor was, indeed and still is, to bend bones and fracture minds. To proclaim the Kingdom as the place where these fractures are healed is to make an open challenge to the norms and patterns of an industrial society. It is also to proclaim the Kingdom as the place where the bent and fractured people, the losers and victims of an industrial society, which uses people up and spits them out, are finally valued, welcomed home, and shown that they belong.

Before we turn to the "turn" of the poem, and the redemption of the phrase "it's a long way off," it is worth observing that as a poet, R.S. Thomas has available to him not simply the paragraph and sentence as units of meaning, but he also has the line: the power and implicit meanings of line breaks and endings; the momentary suspense and renewal when we read to the end of the line, pause, and begin a new one. He makes particularly deft use of line endings in this poem: so we have "the poor man" at the end of line three, left suspended there in his poverty. We don't know what is to become of him until the new line begins with its transformative affirmation "Is king." The line ends with the word is: "the consumptive is." We pause on the brink of this word and the next line ushers us into the Kingdom as it begins with the word "Healed." Again, the next line ends

A Musing on Myths of What and How, a litho by Ryan Stander

with "the blind look." In the pause we don't know whether they still look blindly and blankly, but the new line begins "At themselves." Again, the seventh line ends "industry is for mending." we pause at the line's end not knowing whether this is the mending and repair of the material things with which we associate industry, but the new line transforms the word "mending," for it is not the mending of material things but "The bent bones and the minds fractured." In some ways, these tiny effects, embedded in the details of Thomas's poetic technique, are an epitome of the larger unexpected redemption and transformation which is the true subject of his poem.

The Turn or "Volta"

So, Thomas sets forth a vision of the Kingdom fusing his poetic imagination with the prophetic imagination of scripture. It is an enticing vision, but how do we get there? "It's a long way off," Thomas has declared at the outset of his poem, but now he returns to that phrase and paradoxically offers us a way in:

> ... It's a long way off, but to get
> There takes no time and admission
> Is free,[14]

In the conclusion of his poem, Thomas takes us to a central paradox of the Kingdom itself: on the one hand it is sheer gift, sheer grace, all achieved *for us*, and, if we will let him, achieved *in us* by Christ—"admission is free"; on the other hand to find it, to recognise it, to yearn for it, is to let go of everything else. As T.S. Eliot put it, so tellingly in "Little Gidding," it is

> A condition of complete simplicity
> Costing not less than everything[15]

Here Thomas explores what that means with an image first of purgation and then of faithful presence: "if you purge yourself / of desire and present yourself with / your need only." The distinction between desire and need goes to the heart of the entire critique of industrial consumerism, which this poem has been making. For it is the desire to be king oneself, the desire for supremacy which leaves others bent and fractured. It is the "consumption" of consumerism that must be purged, so that the real need, the need to love and to be loved, which worldliness has masked and numbed, can emerge, be present, and speak clearly.

The last lines of this poem are perfect:

... present yourself with
Your need only and the simple offering
Of your faith, green as a leaf.[16]

"Green as a leaf" might have been a mocking phrase with which the jaded and
sophisticated dismiss the naïve and childlike, but here it is redeemed and summons echoes of Jeremiah's prophetic imagery, on which Edwin Muir also drew:

Blessed is the man that trusteth in the LORD, and whose hope the
LORD is. For he shall be as a tree planted by the waters, and that
spreadeth out her roots by the river, and shall not see when heat
cometh, but her leaf shall be green; and shall not be careful in the
year of drought, neither shall cease from yielding fruit.[17]

Thomas's poem brings us to the brink of the Kingdom and returns us to the
scripture and to Christ with opened eye and heart. Turning from this poem back
to the prophetic strand in scripture, the first thing one should observe is that
the great prophetic writings are themselves poetry of the highest order. When a
prophet is called by God to remind Israel of a covenant, which they have aban-
doned, or to call for a return to that covenant which has not yet been enacted,
the prophets avail themselves of the poetic imagination and offer image after
image to try and body forth the form of things unknown. So it is that a vineyard,
an olive grove, a wine press, a wedding, a feast, a flowering branch of almond,
and a tree planted by the waters are all pressed into service that they might express for us the otherwise inexpressible. But there is more to prophecy than the
embodiment of truth in symbol. When Isaiah prophesies that:

... [God] will destroy on this mountain the shroud that is cast
over all peoples, the sheet that is spread over all nations; he will
swallow up death forever,[18]

Here he offers us an image that goes to the heart of prophecy itself: the
image of unveiling, revealing, taking away the shroud and lifting off the sheet.
When such an unveiling happens there is revelation, a revelation not only of the
hidden forces at work in the present but also a revelation or vision of a fulfilment which has not yet occurred, a vision which is, itself, both a critique of the
present and a source of hope. When Christ began to preach, he was immediately recognised as a prophet in this tradition, and the New Testament is the excit-
ing story of the gradual revelation that he was, and is, so much more than that.
So when we speak of Christ and the Prophetic Imagination we can understand

that phrase in two ways. In one way, of course, we can see in Christ the extraordinary and surprising fulfilment of so much Old Testament prophecy. The Gospels are full of such moments in which an unresolved prophecy, hanging in the air for centuries, suddenly finds its resolution and fulfilment in Christ and the Gospel writer quotes it and exclaims with joy on its fulfilment. The source and epitome of this series of epiphanies in which an Old Testament puzzle suddenly finds its solution, a mysterious prophecy finds its meaning, is the story of the Road to Emmaus, in which Christ shows the forlorn disciples how the very events which they have taken as signs of rejection and defeat, once understood in the light of "Moses and the Prophets" became signs of victory and hope.

Hope vs. Expectation, a charcoal drawing by Craig Hawkins

Then he said to them, "Oh, how foolish you are, and how slow of heart to believe all that the prophets have declared! Was it not necessary that the Messiah should suffer these things and then enter into his glory?" Then beginning with Moses and all the prophets, he interpreted to them the things about himself in all the scriptures.[19]

As the disciples later remark:

They said to each other, "Were not our hearts burning within us …, while he was opening the scriptures to us?"[20]

The realisation that Jesus himself is the fulfilment of prophecy and that the apparent defeat of the cross is revealed or unveiled in the light of the resurrection as victory, completely transforms and galvanises those who grasp it.

But we can see Christ as not only the fulfilment of prophecy, but also as the wielder and kindler of the prophetic imagination. We can see his teaching about the Kingdom and especially his Sermon on the Mount as prophetic in all the senses outlined above: an unveiling, a reversal of fortunes, and a vision of hope. Consider, for example, the Beatitudes. Let us read them again:

Blessed are the poor in spirit, for theirs is the kingdom of heaven.
Blessed are those who mourn, for they will be comforted.
Blessed are the meek, for they will inherit the earth.
Blessed are those who hunger and thirst for righteousness, for they will be filled.
Blessed are the merciful, for they will receive mercy.
Blessed are the pure in heart, for they will see God.
Blessed are the peacemakers, for they will be called children of God.
Blessed are those who are persecuted for righteousness' sake, for theirs is the kingdom of heaven.
Blessed are you when people revile you and persecute you and utter all kinds of evil against you falsely on my account. Rejoice and be glad, for your reward is great in heaven, for in the same way they persecuted the prophets who were before you.[21]

On the face of it this is a set of absurdities and flat contradictions of human experience. We do not experience poverty, mourning, and persecution as blessings. On the face of it, the meek are precisely the people who do not inherit the earth, because the arrogant have, as always, thrust them aside. In ordinary human experience those who dare to act as peacemakers in the midst of conflict, far from being blessed, are cursed and deprecated equally by both sides for daring to suggest a new way of seeing things, and prising people away from the comfort of their familiar hatreds. And yet, in spite of the way they contradict our experience, our hearts leap every time we hear Christ's words. Something in us stirs, some long suppressed hope revives, and we know that Jesus is right.

When I came, in the course of writing *Parable and Paradox*, to make my own response to these over-familiar words, I found that the image which Jesus uses just after he has spoken them—the image of a lantern no longer hidden under a bushel but set on a hill—was, as it were, casting its light back on the sayings themselves, and I came to understand the Beatitudes as a kind of prophetic unveiling. This is how it came out as a sonnet:

The Beatitudes

I bless you, who have spelt your blessings out,
And set this lovely lantern on a hill
Lightening darkness and dispelling doubt
By lifting for a little while the veil.
For longing is the veil of satisfaction,
And grief the veil of future happiness.
I glimpse beneath the veil of persecution
The coming kingdom's overflowing bliss.

Oh, make me pure of heart and help me see,
Amongst the shadows and amidst the mourning,
The promised Comforter, alive and free,
The kingdom coming and the Son returning,
That even in this pre-dawn dark I might
At once reveal and revel in your light.[22]

I firmly believe, indeed it is the core of my Christian hope, that the veil of our mourning will be lifted, that the dark glass through which we presently see will be brightened, that the persecutions and hatreds that seem so rife in our world are not the core, not the deepest truth about the world, but are a veil or shadow covering something better. In the coming of Christ the veil is lifted, lifted not only from the world but also from our own hearts. In Christ we encounter not only what Chesterton called "the buried sunrise of wonder" but also the long-veiled image of God in all his beauty, truth, and goodness. That hidden image is suddenly revealed, through Christ, deep within ourselves and in all the others whom he sends to meet us, in whom he comes to meet us.

So Christ's words here are a promise, a prophecy: "they *will be* comforted, they *will* inherit the earth, they *will* be filled, they will receive mercy, they *will* see God," but his words are also an unveiling and an awakening. In the rest of this chapter, I want to explore how the prophetic imagination, as it is modelled for us in the prophetic writings of scripture, and realised in and through the teachings of Jesus, has itself inspired the imagination of a prophetic writer and artist living nearer our own time, to look at how, in one way or another, the prophetic tradition continues.

Jerusalem: The Emanation of the Giant Albion, detail from plate 92, book and illustrations by William Blake

Blake as a Prophet for Our Times

The writer I want to focus on is William Blake, a poet and artist whom Christians have largely ignored or dismissed as too eccentric and strange to engage with. Blake has been largely left to the attention of New Age adepts and enthusiasts, so much so that you might think that his understandable hostility to the Established Church of his time meant that he was hostile to Christ and the Gospel. Nothing could be further from the truth. There is not space in this book for the detailed and thorough work that needs to be done to show the absolute centrality of Christ and the Gospel in Blake's vision. But let me try, in the space that is left to me, to give you a little flavour of his prophetic writing and make the case that Blake is one of those prophet-poets who can awaken us and bring us back closer to Christ, as our living hope.

For people in Britain the most familiar verses of Blake are the ones we sing in the hymn "Jerusalem," verses, in fact, taken from Blake's longer poem *Milton*. In these verses Blake asks an open question about whether Christ once came to England, as the Glastonbury legend suggests, and asks us imagine how such a vision might kindle us to build Jerusalem afresh in our own society.

Jerusalem

And did those feet in ancient time
Walk upon England's mountains green?
And was the holy Lamb of God
On England's pleasant pastures seen?

And did the Countenance Divine
Shine forth upon our clouded hills?
And was Jerusalem builded here
Among these dark satanic mills?

Bring me my bow of burning gold!
Bring me my arrows of desire!
Bring me my spear! O clouds, unfold!
Bring me my chariot of fire!

I will not cease from mental fight,
Nor shall my sword sleep in my hand,
Till we have built Jerusalem
In England's green and pleasant land.[23]

There are many things happening in this little poem, but one of them is that Blake is trying to do for us, in England, what the prophet Elisha did for the young man in the besieged city as it is told in 2 Kings:

And when the servant of the man of God was risen early, and gone forth, behold, an host compassed the city both with horses and chariots. And his servant said unto him, Alas, my master! how shall we do? And he answered, Fear not: for they that be with us are more than they that be with them. And Elisha prayed, and said, LORD, I pray thee, open his eyes, that he may see. And the LORD opened the eyes of the young man; and he saw: and, behold, the mountain was full of horses and chariots of fire round about Elisha.[24]

Indeed, Blake modelled his prophetic poems on the writings of the major Old Testament prophets, and prefaced the poem *Milton*, from which this lyric is taken, with the words "I would that all God's people were prophets." But for the particular focus of this chapter, I want to take you from this little lyric, which we call "Jerusalem," to the major prophetic poem, which Blake called *Jerusalem: The Emanation of the Giant Albion.* As I am going to be quoting substantially from this poem I should, perhaps, explain a little about the form of Blake's prophetic writings. Blake modelled this and his other great prophetic poems on the form of the prophetic and apocalyptic writings of scripture, and because he was used to reading the scriptures in a many-levelled, partly allegorical, partly typological way, he constructed his own poetry so that it could be read in a similarly multi-layered way. So just as the Bible sometimes speaks of Jerusalem as the actual geographical city but also sometimes speaks of Jerusalem as though she was a woman, a bride of Yahweh, a sister of Judah, so in Blake's poem the character Jerusalem is at one and the same time the new Jerusalem that is to come:

And I John saw the holy city, new Jerusalem, coming down from
God out of heaven, prepared as a bride adorned for her husband.[25]

But "Jerusalem" is also a woman in Blake's story, the "emanation" or other half of the character Albion, who is, amongst other things, a mystical name for England, just as Jerusalem in this poem is a mystical name for England's inner soul. So we can read the story at one level as the tragic tale of how a sensitive and spiritually aware young woman is separated from her guardian and protector and forced to work in a mill, as so many young women in the early nineteenth century actually were. But at another level, and at the same time, we can read it as the story of how England, during the course of the scientific revolution and the Enlightenment, lost touch with its own inner soul, with its capacity for spiritual vision, and became capable of enslaving its own people in the new industries. For the other main character in Blake's poem *Jerusalem*, considered simply as a story, is Albion. And Albion, like Jerusalem, is both a character and an emblem of more than one thing: in the story the character Albion forsakes his emanation Jerusalem and falls into a deep sleep until finally in one of his dreams he realises what he has done and repents. But he is, at the same time, England, the England of the early nineteenth century, that has forsaken inner vision and needs to recover it. The third main character in the story is Christ, sometimes referred to as Jesus, and often simply as "the Lamb." In the story, Jesus finds Jerusalem in her captivity, comforts her and promises to reunite her with Albion, and likewise in the story Jesus rouses Albion, teaches him to remember lost Jerusalem and finally wakes him to new life and light. But we can see immediately how all these actions in the plot of the story are telling us about

England's apostasy and also prophesying England's recovery. Jesus is both a character in Blake's story and also the risen Christ, standing beside him as he composes the prophecy and beside us as we read it.

But there is another deeper and more universal level to Blake's writing in this book. For although at one level he is writing about Albion as the type or mythological personage who represents England, he is also, through this specific instance of one nation's apostasy, speaking about all of humanity, as he says in the poem, "I see the Four fold Man. The Humanity in deadly sleep." Here again Blake is following the Bible and a deep hermeneutical tradition, in which episodes in the story of the Old Testament, such as Israel's exile in Babylon, are seen to be the story not only of one nation, but to be emblems or expressions of what has become of all humanity, in the bondage of sin. A further element of which we need to be aware, is that Blake also introduces into his poetry certain allegorical or archetypal figures unique to his imagination, part of his personal mythology. The one that will concern us here is a figure whom Blake calls "Los" and who represents the creative or artistic imagination, and the liberating and clarifying role of the arts in the world.

As we will see, Blake is making an important point when Albion tells Christ that he first glimpsed him "in the likeness and similitude of Los." In other Words Blake is saying that it is the creative arts, the works of imagination which may first arouse people from their deadly slumber, also awaken them spiritually, and eventually bring them to Christ. Finally, we need to remember that Blake is a great visual artist, as well as an inspired poet, and that these prophetic poems were not produced as texts to be printed out in the normal way, but engraved by Blake in his own handwriting on copper plates and surrounded by images and illustrations of his own design. He printed these plates out and then hand-coloured the illustrations. This has a powerful effect on how we read the text.

If we want to know from Blake himself what was trying to achieve in this poem and how he hoped to achieve it, then we should hear these remarkable words from Blake's own "Preface" (from plate 4, seen on the next page):

Preface to Jerusalem
Trembling I sit day and night, my friends are astonish'd at me.
Yet they forgive my wanderings, I rest not from my great task!
To open the Eternal Worlds, to open the immortal Eyes
Of Man inwards into the Worlds of Thought: into Eternity
Ever expanding in the Bosom of God. the Human Imagination
O Saviour pour upon me thy Spirit of meekness & love:
Annihilate the Selfhood in me, be thou all my life![26]

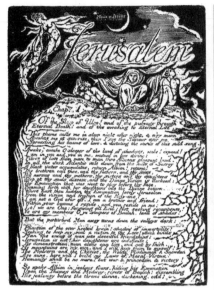 

Jerusalem: The Emanation of the Giant Albion, plate 4 (left) and plate 5 (right)

Here he simultaneously invokes the human imagination and Christ himself, as Saviour to assist him in the essential prophetic task of opening worlds, opening eyes. And when he looks at the England of his day, the England of the early nineteenth century, with prophetic eyes, what does he see? He sees:

> Abstract Philosophy warring in enmity against Imagination
> (Which is the Divine Body of the Lord Jesus. blessed for ever).[27]

Having set its theme, the poem takes the form of a vision in which humanity and, more particularly, an England in the grip of materialism and imperial ambition is "figured" as a sleeping giant called "Albion," who has closed his eyes to the reality of Christ and is instead dreaming, and tragically enacting the nightmare of industrial revolution and imperial aggression:

> I see the Four-fold Man. The Humanity in deadly sleep
> And its fallen Emanation. The Spectre & its cruel Shadow.
> I see the Past, Present & Future, existing all at once
> Before me; O Divine Spirit sustain me on thy wings!
> That I may awake Albion from his long & cold repose.
> For Bacon & Newton sheathd in dismal steel, their terrors hang
> Like iron scourges over Albion, Reasonings like vast Serpents
> Infold around my limbs, bruising my minute articulations[28]

In the hymn "Jerusalem," we heard Blake refer to "those dark satanic mills" and these are popularly assumed to be the newly mechanised mills of the Industrial Revolution. In fact, Blake meant a great deal more than that. He saw that the mechanised mills in which people themselves were reduced to being cogs in a machine were themselves the product of an earlier mechanisation of thought—a Newtonian mechanical model of the universe and almost behaviouristic psychology and economics from Locke, Hume, and others, as he goes on to say in the next lines of his prophecy:

> I turn my eyes to the Schools & Universities of Europe
> And there behold the Loom of Locke whose Woof rages dire
> Washd by the Water-wheels of Newton. black the cloth
> In heavy wreathes folds over every Nation; cruel Works
> Of many Wheels I view, wheel without wheel, with cogs tyrannic
> Moving by compulsion each other: not as those in Eden: which
> Wheel within Wheel in freedom revolve in harmony & peace.[29]

You will see that in these lines, Blake evokes the same passage in Isaiah that we have already cited, which describes a black cloth "in heavy wreaths and folds over every nation." And, of course, to allude to that prophecy is to summon the hope given by Isaiah that God will

> ... destroy on this mountain the shroud that is cast over all peoples, the sheet that is spread over all nations; he will swallow up death forever.[30]

How is that to happen? In Blake's view it can happen only through repentance, and through a new encounter with Christ. Let us look at three key moments in the allegory of Blake's poem. In the first, Christ himself seeks, within the dream, to waken the sleeping Albion through the prophetic utterance of Blake himself:

> Awake! Awake O sleeper of the land of shadows, wake! expand!
> I am in you and you in me, mutual in love divine:
> Fibres of love from man to man thro Albions pleasant land.[31]

Here Blake imagines Christ speaking in the words to which Paul bears witness in Ephesians:

but everything exposed by the light becomes visible, for everything
that becomes visible is light. Therefore it says,
> "Sleeper, awake!
> Rise from the dead,
> and Christ will shine on you."[32]

But at this stage in the poem, Albion refuses the call of grace and turns away
into darkness, denying the divine reality and seeking instead a path of division,
possession, and power:

> But the perturbed Man away turns down the valleys dark . . .
> Phantom of the over heated brain! shadow of immortality!
> Seeking to keep my soul a victim to thy Love! which binds
> Man the enemy of man into deceitful friendships;
> Jerusalem is not! her daughters are indefinite;
> By demonstration, man alone can live, and not by faith.[33]

So here Albion rejects Jesus and seeks to reduce the mystery of faith to
mere biological phenomena, the firing of neurons, "phantom of the over heated
brain." And this is historically what was happening in Britain in Blake's lifetime
in the gradual decline from theism into deism, from deism into mere materialism. And this decline was accompanied, as we saw earlier, by a rejection of the
imagination and an irrational reliance on reason in its narrowest form alone:

> By demonstration, man alone can live, and not by faith.[34]

But to understand the next key moment in Blake's narrative we must open
out that strange line

> Jerusalem is not! her daughters are indefinite;[35]

Jerusalem in this poem, is Albion's emanation and his bride, she is his true
spiritual self, so to seek separation from her, and even to deny her existence, is to
live as though we had no soul, and Blake saw that that was precisely what modern society was trying to do. But Blake is not just concerned with what the loss of
Jerusalem does to Albion, he is concerned with what becomes of Jerusalem herself. When she is separated from him at this moment she becomes a prisoner in
Babylon and it will have to be Jesus himself who rescues her, and reunites them.
In a passage of great prophetic insight, Blake describes Jerusalem's captivity in
terms that could equally describe the young girls who were being pressed into

virtual slavery to work in the mills of the Industrial Revolution. Blake prefaces this passage in his poem with the line:

This is the Song of the Lamb, sung by Slaves in evening time.

And this is how Blake describes the scene

But Jerusalem faintly saw him, closd in the Dungeons of Babylon
Her Form was held by Beulahs Daughters. but all within unseen
She sat at the Mills, her hair unbound her feet naked
Cut with the flints: her tears run down, her reason grows like
The Wheel of Hand. incessant turning day & night without rest
Insane she raves upon the winds hoarse, inarticulate:
All night Vala hears. she triumphs in pride of holiness
To see Jerusalem deface her lineaments with bitter blows
Of despair.[36]

We can see that Jerusalem herself is about to give up and lose her vision: "her reason grows like the wheel of Hand." Blake in a prophetic insight seems to foresee the tragic phenomenon of self-harm which we see in so many young women in our own society, whom we have condemned, like Jerusalem here, to live in an inhuman system governed by an inhuman philosophy.

But this is not the end of the story, even though it appears to represent the place where we are presently stuck as a society. And this is where, having unveiled the horrors of the present situation, Blake, like all great prophets, goes on to restore hope, to look to the future that Christ has for us. For in Blake's vision Jerusalem, even in her exile, is not alone:

But the Divine Lamb stood beside Jerusalem. oft she saw
The lineaments Divine & oft the Voice heard, & oft she said:
O Lord & Saviour, have the Gods of the Heathen pierced thee?
Or hast thou been pierced in the House of thy Friends?
Art thou alive! & livest thou for-evermore? or art thou
Not: but a delusive shadow, a thought that liveth not.
Babel mocks saying, there is no God nor Son of God
That thou O Human Imagination, O Divine Body art all
A delusion. but I know thee O Lord when thou arisest upon
My weary eyes even in this dungeon & this iron mill...[37]
Thus spake Jerusalem, & thus the Divine Voice replied.
Mild Shade of Man, pitiest thou these Visions of terror & woe!

> Give forth thy pity & love. fear not! lo I am with thee always.
> Only believe in me that I have power to raise from death
> Thy Brother who Sleepeth in Albion:[38]

This is an extraordinary and intimate exchange. It is not the *power* of God that pierces and reaches through to Jerusalem in her exile but it is rather his *weakness*. She realises that in Christ, God himself has been pierced like her:

> O Lord & Saviour, have the Gods of the Heathen pierced thee?
> Or hast thou been pierced in the House of thy Friends?[39]

That last question is exceptionally poignant, for it is not just that Jesus was indeed pierced in the house of his friends, betrayed with a kiss, and crucified by people he came to save, but also that he continues to be re-crucified even by his own church in their attitudes to the poor and excluded.

But Jerusalem sees him at last, and lays before him all the doubts which sceptical materialism has inflicted on her.

> Art thou alive! & livest thou for-evermore? or art thou
> Not: but a delusive shadow, a thought that liveth not.
> Babel mocks saying, there is no God nor Son of God
> That thou O Human Imagination, O Divine Body art all
> A delusion.[40]

The awakened and awakening presence of Christ is enough to dispel these doubts:

> but I know thee O Lord when thou arisest upon
> My weary eyes even in this dungeon & this iron mill ...[41]

And Jesus replies to her, first with words drawn directly from the end of Matthew's Gospel and then with a promise that even Albion himself will recover:

> lo I am with thee always.
> Only believe in me that I have power to raise from death
> Thy Brother who Sleepeth in Albion:[42]

After this secret encounter between Christ and Jerusalem, who is Albion's inner soul, Blake returns us to Albion himself. We had left Albion at the moment when he turned aside and was separated from Jerusalem. And that is perhaps

Jerusalem: The Emanation of the Giant Albion, plate 62 (detail)

where
England was when
Blake was writing. But it is not the end of the poem.
Here's what happens next. Albion, not yet awoken, sees the
shallowness, the chaff, the destruction of his alienated life:

> O what is Life & what is Man. O what is Death? Wherefore
> Are you my Children. natives in the Grave to where I go
> Or are you born to feed the hungry ravenings of Destruction
> To be the sport of Accident! to waste in Wrath & Love, a weary
> Life. in brooding cares & anxious labours, that prove but chaff.[43]

And then at last he remembers Jerusalem, the hidden spiritual core of his
life, whom he has forsaken:

> O Jerusalem Jerusalem I have forsaken thy Courts
> … thy Gates of Thanksgiving thy Windows of Praise:
> Thy Clouds of Blessing; thy Cherubims of Tender-mercy
> Stretching their Wings sublime over the Little-ones of Albion[44]

And at last he repents, and in his dream he sees Christ with outstretched
arms and turns back to him:

> O Human Imagination O Divine Body I have Crucified
> I have turned my back upon thee into the Wastes of Moral Law:
> There Babylon is builded in the Waste. founded in Human
> desolation.[45]

The key moment of this repentance comes in the last lines of this passage
I have just quoted, in which Albion not only turns to address Christ but recognises that Christ himself is the bodying forth of that imagination, which heals
the divide in our minds and reconciles our intuition and reason. Furthermore,
Albion recognises that in rejecting and crucifying the imagination he has

crucified Christ, and in crucifying Christ he has crucified his own inner imaginative life and soul and constructed instead a system and religion of mere
moralism, riddled with hypocrisy:

Jerusalem: The Emanation of the Giant Albion, plate 76

O Human Imagination O Divine Body I have Crucified
I have turned my back upon thee into the Wastes of Moral Law.[46]

Albion sees Christ crucified and yet radiant, not on a cross but on the tree of life, and Albion spreads his own arms, cruciform and yet open in praise in a gesture of recognition.

This act of repentance means that at last Albion can truly awaken. Blake describes this awakening beautifully, in lines that echo the hymn "Jerusalem" that we sing:

> The Breath Divine went forth upon the morning hills, Albion mov'd
> Upon the Rock. he opend his eyelids in pain; in pain he mov'd
> His stony members, he saw England. Ah! shall the Dead live again
> The Breath Divine went forth over the morning hills Albion rose[47]

So at last Albion and Jesus meet in the waking world:

> Then Jesus appeared standing by Albion as the Good Shepherd
> By the lost Sheep that he hath found & Albion knew that it
> Was the Lord the Universal Humanity, & Albion saw his Form
> A Man. & they conversed as Man with Man, in Ages of Eternity
> And the Divine Appearance was the likeness & similitude of Los[48]

Remember in Blake's mythology, Los is the figure who represents creativity and the imaginative arts, so Jesus appears to Albion as the divine artist!

Recognising the signs of the passion Albion asks Jesus:

> Cannot Man exist without Mysterious
> Offering of Self for Another, is this Friendship & Brotherhood
> I see thee in the likeness and similitude of Los my Friend[49]

And Jesus replies:

> Wouldest thou love one who never died
> For thee or ever die for one who had not died for thee
> And if God dieth not for Man & giveth not himself
> Eternally for Man Man could not exist. for Man is Love:
> As God is Love: every kindness to another is a little Death
> In the Divine Image nor can Man exist but by Brotherhood[50]

Jerusalem is a work of prophetic imagination, and as such it dares to peer over the event-horizon, it takes us further than we have actually travelled. Looking around at our society now, in the midst of an ecological crisis brought on by our polluting industries and gross consumerism, in the midst of a mental health crisis brought on by our cold, alienating philosophies, and a way of life that amounts to institutionalised anomie, in the midst of a moral crisis that sees us exploiting one another economically, sexually, and in almost every other way, we seem still to be in that part of the prophecy in which "the cruel works of many wheels" grind on, in which the "cogs tyrannic move each other by compulsion" not by love, in which our own spiritual lives are still "In the Dungeons of Babylon, cut with flints," "defacing our own lineaments with bitter blows." Blake is a great prophet because he reveals that reality to us, but he is a greater prophet still because he does not end his prophecy there—he is faithful to Jesus and he knows there is resurrection, the dead shall live again. So when Albion awakens Jesus says to him:

> Fear not Albion unless I die thou canst not live
> But if I die I shall arise again & thou with me[51]

Blake's poem, and all prophetic art, is intended to arouse us and stir us to action. How do we awake from the deadly sleep? How do we throw off the folds of the heavy black cloth? How do we lift the veil?

NOTES

1 Walter Bruegemann (b. 1933) is an academic and Old Testament scholar who wrote *The Prophetic Imagination* (Minneapolis, MN: Fortress Press, 1978).

2 R.S. Thomas, "The Kingdom," in *H'm* (New York: Macmillan, 1972), p. 34.

3 Ibid.

4 Ibid.

5 Ibid.

6 Ibid.

7 Ibid.

8 Matthew 11:2–5.

9 Luke 4:18–21.

10 Ecclesiastes 1:2–3 (KJV).

11 Thomas, "The Kingdom," p. 34.

12 1 Corinthians 13:12 (KJV).

13 It is very heartening to see some resistance and reaction to this now, as the environmental catastrophe being brought on by so much waste is leading people to ask for things that last and to set up their own local "Repair Cafes" to mend what is broken.

14 Thomas, "The Kingdom," p. 34.

15 T.S. Eliot, "Little Gidding," from *Four Quartets*, in *T.S. Eliot: The Complete Poems and Plays* (London, UK: Faber, 1969), p. 198.

16 Ibid.

17 Jeremiah 17:7–8 (KJV).

18 Isaiah 25:6–8.

19 Luke 24:25–27.

20 Luke 24:32.

21 Matthew 5:3–12

22 Malcolm Guite, "The Beatitudes," in *Parable and Paradox: Sonnets on the Sayings of Jesus and Other Poems* (London, UK: Canterbury Press, 2016), p. 30.

23 The English hymn "Jerusalem" is text taken from the preface to William Blake's poem *Milton* (1808), set to music by Sir Hubert Parry in 1916.

24 2 Kings 6:15–17 (KJV, as used by William Blake).

25 Revelation 21:2 (KJV).

26 William Blake, *Jerusalem: the Emanation of the Giant Albion*, from *The Complete Poetry and Prose of William Blake*, ed. by David V. Erdman (Berkeley, CA: University of California Press, 1982), p. 147, plate 5, lines 16–22.

27 Blake, Jerusalem, p. 148, plate 5, lines 58–59.

28 Blake, p. 159, plate 15, lines 6–13.

29 Ibid., lines 16–20.

30 Isaiah 25:6–8.

31 Blake, Jerusalem, p. 146, plate 4, lines 6–8.

32 Ephesians 5: 13–14.

33 Blake, Jerusalem, pp. 146–147, plate 4, lines 22–28.

34 Ibid., line 28.

35 Blake, pp. 146–147, plate 60, line 38.

36 Blake, pp. 210–211, plate 60, lines 39–47.

37 Blake, p. 211, plate 60, lines 50–59.

38 Ibid., lines 65–69

39   Ibid., lines 52–53.

40   Ibid., lines 54–58.

41   Ibid., lines 58–59.

42   Ibid., lines 67–69.

43   Blake, p. 169, plate 24, line 16.

44   Ibid., lines 17 and 20–23.

45   Ibid., lines 23–25.

46   Ibid., lines 18–19.

47   Blake, pp. 254–255, plate 95, lines 2–5.

48   Blake, p. 255, plate 96, lines 3–7.

49   Blake, p. 256, plate 96, lines 20–22.

50   Ibid., lines 23–28.

51   Blake, p. 255, plate 96, lines 14–15.

WILLIAM BLAKE WRITES in his prose address to the Christians embedded in the poem *Jerusalem*:

> I know of no other Christianity and of no other Gospel than the liberty both of body and mind to exercise the Divine Arts of Imagination.[1]

You remember that at the outset of the book we said that "From the first moment that he proclaims the Kingdom of God, Jesus appeals to our imagination." It is just this imagination, to which Jesus appeals, that helps us to lift the veil, or rather allows us to let Christ and the gift of his Spirit begin to lift it for us and in us. This is not to say that the imagination, left to itself, and separated from its roots in the the loving communion of the Trinity, cannot sometimes be dark, shadowed, or misleading. All things are shadowed in this fallen world and the best in us, severed from our roots in God, and in the divine image we bear, can become corrupted and misleading. But this is not a council of despair. We cannot abandon the imagination God has given us because we are sometimes afraid of it. Rather we need what C.S. Lewis called "a baptised Imagination." And sometimes, for some artists (and I include myself amongst them), the imagination is baptised first, and the rest of us just takes a little longer to catch up! Lewis felt that by a kind of prevenient grace his imagination came to be baptised when he read George MacDonald as a teenager. Even though he was, in his head, still an atheist, his heart was already being won over by the baptised imagination of MacDonald, a great Christian mytho-poeic writer whose book *Phantastes* began, on that famous train journey, to lift the veil for Lewis, so that he not only fell in love with the glory and holiness he found in the book, but that also that "luminous cloud," as he called it, seemed to move from the book to the world, from art to life, and show him, unveiled, the beauty and holiness of the woods and groves of Surrey as they went by the train windows.

And I Knew It Not, a linocut by Matthew Clark and Ned Bustard

For Lewis that baptism of imagination was a sheer gift of grace, unlooked for at the time, a kind of surprise, a divinely given stab of joy. But later, when he came fully to faith, he took care to bring his imagination constantly back to its source in Christ, to pray about his work, to offer it to God for blessing and sometimes for correction. As artists we can do the same, and if we do, it might be that one of our stories, one of our poems and paintings might meet with some young atheist, some C.S. Lewis of the future, and baptise their imagination too!

And if we do that, if we make a baptised imagination available to Christ for the spiritual work of lifting the veil, then we will find ourselves taking our part in one of the great works of resistance and liberation in our time. It is by the divine art of imagination that we resist the forces at work in our own age: forces of materialism and reductivism that have cast the film of familiarity, "the veil of the ordinary," over God's world, a world that is, in fact, still radiant with his glory, a glory that the modern, western mindset of domination and materialism has veiled from us.

Head of Christ, a woodcut by Edward Knippers

I believe this imaginative resistance, this imaginative lifting of the veil, has already begun and is already starting to transform the church. The divided worlds of reason and imagination are beginning to be knit back together as C.S. Lewis longed that they should be. The emergence of centres for theology and the arts in the great universities, the emergence of groups like the

Opening the Fold, an etching by Samuel Palmer

Rabbit Room and CIVA (Christians in the Visual Arts), the existence of presses like Square Halo Books that have brought you this book—all these, I believe, are part of a broader stirring, a turning of the tide, an awakening.

Throughout this book I have been making the case for the imagination as a truth-bearing faculty, and as an essential element in our coming to Christ and his coming to us. I have distinguished between three aspects of the imagination: the *poetic*, the *moral*, and the *prophetic*, but, as Coleridge said, it is the philosopher's privilege to distinguish but not to divide. For these three are one! When the *poetic* imagination removes the film of familiarity, when it rinses and cleanses the source of our seeing, and reveals breathtaking beauty in Christ and the world he loves, we respond to beauty with a longing for goodness. The *poetic* imagination does not simply rouse the *moral* imagination: it *becomes* it.

And when beauty has aroused the desire for the good then the same poetic imagination that removed the film of familiarity and restored wonder, now becomes the *prophetic* imagination and lifts the veil of time itself, lifts up the heavy black cloth of history, and gives a vision of the eschaton, the end and fulfillment of things, the kingdom come, and the earth filled with "the glory of the LORD, as the waters cover the sea."[2]

And that gives us hope! Hope is the church's great gift to the world and its great strength. The world itself has almost no hope at all, but we have abundant hope in Christ, and not just in Christ's final coming, but right now,

"Christ in you, the hope of glory."[3]

God has many ways of lifting the veil, many ways of encouraging his church, many ways of rousing the world from its deadly slumber, but it is my conviction that one of those ways, one of the most effective and salient ways in our time, is by kindling our imaginations, by speaking to us through the poets, the storytellers, the playwrights, the artists, the filmmakers, by opening our eyes afresh to the rich poetry of scripture itself.

In this book I hope I have made the case for an imaginative grasp of faith and an imaginative proclamation of that faith, and most of all for a glad recognition that in Christ, our imagination, in all its modes and forms, is baptised and renewed.

So I want to end this book by renewing Blake's address to the Christians with a specific call to action, a call to all of you who are artists, poets, musicians, photographers, filmmakers, dramatists, kindlers of the imagination in yourselves and others. A call to take up afresh the great task as Blake called it:

> To open the Eternal Worlds, to open the immortal Eyes
> Of Man inwards into the Worlds of Thought: into Eternity
> Ever expanding in the Bosom of God. the Human Imagination[4]

Blake follows those words with a two line prayer, which might be the prayer of any Christian artist taking up the task, beginning their work afresh, in our own day. I end this book with the same prayer:

> O Saviour pour upon me thy Spirit of meekness & love:
> Annihilate the Selfhood in me, be thou all my life![5]

NOTES

1   William Blake, *Jerusalem: The Emanation of the Giant Albion,* from *The Complete Poetry and Prose of William Blake,* ed. David V. Erdman (Berkeley, CA: University of California Press, 1982), p. 231, plate 77.

2   Habakkuk 2:14.

3   Colossians 1:27.

4   Blake, *Jerusalem,* p. 147, plate 5, lines 18–20.

5   Ibid., lines 21–22.

MORE BOOKS *for* *the* IMAGINATION

NAMING THE ANIMALS:
AN INVITATION TO CREATIVITY

"A lovely primer about our collective call to be creative. Accessible to all, Roach and Bustard's book sets readers on a path toward deeper exploration into the role of creativity within our Christian walk." —Lawan Glasscock, Christians in the Visual Arts (CIVA)

IT WAS GOOD: PERFORMING ARTS
TO THE GLORY OF GOD

". . . a wise book written by experienced practitioners who have been in the trenches of creating art from a Christian worldview. It ain't easy, and if you want to try it, I suggest that you read this book." —Max McLean, founder of the Fellowship for Performing Arts

TEACHING BEAUTY: A VISION FOR
MUSIC & ART IN CHRISTIAN EDUCATION

"*Teaching Beauty* is a must-read for school administrators, teachers, education majors, and all who seek to encourage the next generation to engage in creativity and beauty." —Robert F. Bigley, The Trust Performing Arts Center

J.R.R. TOLKIEN AND THE ARTS:
A THEOLOGY OF SUBCREATION

"This collection of writings about Tolkien's life and work as an artist (in the broad sense) who was also a committed Christian, is a welcome companion for anyone looking for ways to understand and articulate their own creative theology under the loving gaze of a Creator." —Andrew Peterson, author, singer/songwriter, and founder of The Rabbit Room

SQUAREHALOBOOKS.com